Unpack Harmful Dynamics from Your
Childhood, Empower Yourself As an Adult,
and Set Boundaries for the Future

EMOTIONALLY IMMATURE PARENTS:
A Recovery Workbook for Adult Children

Kai Tai Kevin Qiu, MD
@hicoachkai

ADAMS MEDIA
NEW YORK   LONDON   TORONTO   SYDNEY   NEW DELHI

Adams Media
An Imprint of Simon & Schuster, Inc.
100 Technology Center Drive
Stoughton, Massachusetts 02072

First Adams Media trade paperback edition October 2023

For information about special discounts for bulk purchases, please contact Simon & Schuster Special Sales at 1-866-506-1949 or business@simonandschuster.com.

The Simon & Schuster Speakers Bureau can bring authors to your live event. For more information or to book an event, contact the Simon & Schuster Speakers Bureau at 1-866-248-3049 or visit our website at www.simonspeakers.com.

Interior design by Colleen Cunningham

Manufactured in the United States of America

1 2023

Library of Congress Cataloging-in-Publication Data
Names: Qiu, Kai Tai Kevin, author.
Title: Emotionally immature parents: a recovery workbook for adult children / Kai Tai Kevin Qiu, MD.
Description: Stoughton, Massachusetts: Adams Media, [2023]
Identifiers: LCCN 2023024744 | ISBN 9781507221174 (pb) | ISBN 9781507222294 (ebook)
Subjects: LCSH: Parent and child. | Adult children--Psychology. | Adult children of dysfunctional families. | Emotional deprivation. | Psychic trauma--Treatment.
Classification: LCC BF723.P25 Q58 2023 | DDC 155.9/24--dc23/eng/20230624
LC record available at https://lccn.loc.gov/2023024744

ISBN 978-1-5072-2117-4
ISBN 978-1-5072-2229-4 (ebook)

Contents

Preface

HELPING PEOPLE HEAL FROM THEIR emotionally immature parents, create healthier relationships, and live an authentic life is a mission that's near and dear to my heart. I was once (and I still am) a son who is healing from my childhood wounds and working on my relationship with my parents. I understand and have felt the loneliness, confusion, frustration, anger, resentment, sadness, burden, guilt, and shame of growing up with emotionally immature parents. It was a painful experience. I wished there was an adult who could've been there for me and guided me through those challenging years. I wished I hadn't had to grow up so soon, play the parent for my parents, survive through the chaos, or deal with adult issues that I wasn't equipped to deal with.

For the past ten years I've been on a journey of self-discovery and healing. I'm immensely grateful for the guides, the teachers, the mentors, the therapists, the doctors, the coaches, and the supportive friends and family who have taught me so much along the way. I wouldn't be here today without them. Now I focus on being that guiding support that I didn't have when I was younger. As a certified life coach with a background in psychiatric care, I provide coaching, courses, and virtual events in the aim of being that change for others. I want to help others learn that they can overcome their challenges and live an emotionally fulfilling life. So, let's get healing.

Introduction

WERE YOU TAUGHT AS A CHILD to keep your emotions bottled up? Do you struggle to recall a time when your parent apologized for something they did or said that hurt you? Growing up, did you often find yourself stuck in a role—caretaker, peacemaker, rebel—that you didn't choose for yourself? If so, you might have been a child raised by an emotionally immature parent. An emotionally immature parent is one who has limited capacities for emotional intimacy, empathy, self-reflection, and emotional regulation. Growing up with an emotionally immature parent, you may have felt lonely and unseen, and these experiences can still affect you today. Maybe you continue the cycle of avoiding emotions in intimate connections or feel shame in just thinking about taking care of yourself.

In order to fully enjoy the present in your current relationships, experience a deep sense of self-worth and belonging, and create a happier future, it is essential to heal from your experiences with an emotionally immature parent. *Emotionally Immature Parents: A Recovery Workbook for Adult Children* is your guide to this healing. Here, you will discover a greater understanding of your emotionally immature parent(s), validation for your past and current experiences, and actionable steps to recovery.

In Part 1, you will find out more about what it means to be emotionally immature and the signs of an emotionally immature parent. You will dig deeper into the ways you were impacted as a child—and how those effects show up today. You will also take the first steps toward healing by learning about the importance of boundaries and mindful practices like meditation. Then, in Parts 2 and 3, you will follow over seventy interactive activities to help you accept the past, embrace the present, and manifest a joyful future. You'll:

- Become a curious detective of your childhood experiences.

- Express the difficult feelings.

- Let go of self-defeating beliefs.

- Ask for what you want and need.

- Build safe and respectful connections.

- And so much more.

As you journey through this workbook, you will be able to see your parent more objectively in order to have more enjoyable interactions or make the decision to limit contact, depending on what is best for you. You will learn how to love yourself just as you are and become emotionally mature by accessing, regulating, and expressing your true feelings—bringing you closer in your most intimate relationships. As you take these steps in healing, go slowly, and give each activity the time and attention it calls for. Be patient with the journey and with yourself. Let's begin…

PART 1

RECOGNIZING EMOTIONALLY IMMATURE PARENTS AND THEIR EFFECTS

Why is it that you feel unsatisfied after a conversation with your father? Why do you often feel like you and your mother are one person rather than two unique individuals? In this part, you will find the answers to these questions and more. You'll explore emotional immaturity and the characteristics of an emotionally immature parent. You'll also reflect on the emotional difficulties of growing up with an emotionally immature parent as well as the more long-term effects these experiences can have on your adult emotions and relationships. Then you'll take the first steps toward healing by discovering the importance of healthy boundaries and what they look like, how self-awareness opens the door to change, and what kinds of self-awareness practices you will find in Parts 2 and 3. You'll start doing the inner work that will continue throughout this book.

Having a deeper understanding about your parent, yourself, your childhood experiences, and the challenges that you face today, in addition to the self-awareness tools that will help you grow and heal, will give you greater power and freedom in how you navigate difficult interactions in the future. With this knowledge, you can begin cultivating the healthy relationships you deserve.

CHAPTER 1

Understanding Emotionally Immature Parents

Emotional immaturity encompasses several traits, including low emotional intelligence and resilience, poor emotional recognition and regulation, lack of capacity for empathy, differing degrees of self-centeredness with limited self-reflection, a discomfort and fear of experiencing emotions, discomfort with others expressing their genuine emotions, and an inability to communicate and express emotions. In this chapter, you will learn more about what it looks like when a parent is emotionally immature, from a deeper look into these traits to how they may show up in real life. You will then explore how these traits affected your childhood experiences. Though a parent may be trying their best, the limitations of emotional immaturity prevent them from being able to be emotionally intimate with their children. For example, they may struggle to pick up on when their child is upset and relate to those upset feelings. In reflecting on the past, you can uncover insight into which limitations may have affected your relationship with your parent more than others and what limitations you might not have recognized as such previously.

What Is Emotional Maturity?

Before getting into the characteristics of an emotionally immature parent and how they impacted you as a child, it's important to first understand what it looks like when a person *has* emotional maturity. This person is comfortable with experiencing their own emotions. They are able to monitor, assess, and regulate how they're feeling and also recognize, monitor, assess, and help others regulate how they're feeling. They are interested in others' feelings and allow others to express these feelings. They're capable of empathy and taking on someone else's perspective, and they feel called to help and support others in building a deeper social and emotional connection.

An emotionally mature person has a solid sense of their identity and uses internal resources like self-love, self-acceptance, and self-encouragement to feel safe and secure within themselves. They seek emotional intimacy and depth in their relationships. They want to genuinely relate with others, get to know them, and understand them for who they are. Others feel safe, seen, appreciated, respected, and cared for when around them.

While an emotionally immature parent has the characteristics highlighted in the next section, an emotionally mature parent sits at the other end of the spectrum. Of course, even an emotionally mature parent may slip up and be reactive from time to time and in certain situations. No one is perfect. The difference is that they will self-reflect, take ownership for their behavior, listen to how their actions might've made you feel, try to be better next time, and apologize and make amends if necessary.

Characteristics of an Emotionally Immature Parent

Though you likely weren't aware as a child, there are names for the behaviors you noticed in your parent when you were growing up. The following is a list of the primary characteristics of an emotionally immature parent, including details about how these traits can show up in real-life situations. You can add a check mark next to the traits that most reflect your experiences growing up.

- **Self-centeredness.** They aren't interested in your inner experiences, your interests, your struggles, and your life. Conversations always lead back to them. The relationship feels very one-sided, draining, and unsatisfying.

- **Lack of empathy and understanding.** Their self-centeredness, their discomfort and fear in feeling their own feelings, and their inability to tune into their emotions makes it impossible for them to be there for you on an emotional level. You can't give what you don't have, and they don't have the capacity to truly understand how you are feeling. This creates dissatisfying, superficial, and frustrating interactions where you feel like they don't care about you or even know who you really are.

- **Lack of self-awareness and self-reflection.** They are unaware of, and have little interest in examining, their inner world of thoughts, feelings, perspectives, and beliefs. They do not reflect on how their behaviors and what they say affect others. Their lack of self-reflection can make it hard for them to learn from their mistakes and make the necessary changes and adjustments to improve their relationships with themselves and others.

- **Intense and reactive emotions.** They express outbursts of emotions with a lack of self-control. These outbursts can feel very unexpected to those around them.

- **Impulsiveness and insensitivity.** It's difficult for them to think before speaking or acting, especially when they're experiencing charged emotions or strong opinions. They can even pride themselves on speaking their mind without thinking about how it affects others. If they're called out for saying something hurtful, they'll dismiss it, make excuses, or call you sensitive and emotional.

- **Discomfort with experiencing their own genuine emotions.** They are uncomfortable and even afraid of experiencing their emotions. They unconsciously feel ashamed and bad for feeling certain emotions like anger and sadness.

- **Discomfort with other people's emotions and emotional needs.** Since they're unable to get in touch with their own feelings and are uncomfortable even trying, they lack interest in listening to you talk about your emotions, and they are unable to provide you with emotional support in your times of need.

- **Low stress tolerance.** They aren't skilled in coping with stress. They can easily get overwhelmed, shut down, avoid issues, or take a passive-aggressive approach to dealing with problems. They rely on others to manage their stress levels; others are there to rescue and save them from their stress, and if they're unavailable or unable to, they're seen as abandoners.

- **Rigid black-and-white thinking.** It's either their way or the highway. Their opinions are always right, and they're unwilling to hear your opinion. Or, if they do hear it, they're unwilling to learn and see from your perspective. They struggle with the concept of "let's agree to disagree."

- **Unspoken expectations and use of phrases like, "If you really love me…"** They expect others to read their minds and give them what they want and need instead of directly asking for what they want and need. It can get extra confusing when they sometimes don't even know what it is that they need, but they still have the unspoken expectation for others around them of, "If you really love me, you will give me what I need and make me feel good even though I don't know what I need right now."

- **Nonassertive (defensive, passive-aggressive, passive) patterns of dealing with issues.** They fear conflicts and confrontations, possibly because they themselves grew up in a volatile, emotionally cold, and unsafe environment. As a child, they likely witnessed conflicts turn into loud, possibly physical fights.

- **Inability or refusal to apologize and make amends.** Since they lack self-reflection, they don't think about their part in relationship issues. They cannot stand making a mistake or admitting to being wrong because they want to avoid experiencing shame. For them, owning a mistake means that they're a bad person rather than that what they did was bad and a lesson in what to change in the future. They expect others to always apologize and make amends.

- **Self-esteem dependent on getting what they want.** When they want something from you, they want it *now*. They'll feel good about themselves and about you if you can help them, but if you can't, they'll feel even more upset and take it personally. Once again, they see others as either rescuers or abandoners.

- **Lack of a sense of own identity.** Because they lack self-awareness and thus personal development, they do not have a firm sense of their own identity, desires, interests, and needs. Instead, they're constantly requiring others to validate and approve of them, make choices for them, and save them (or they assume the identity of savior for someone else).

- **Rigid family roles.** They believe that everyone in the family plays a specific role with specific expectations and behaviors. Everything is standardized as either good or bad, and there's a right way of doing things and a wrong way of doing things. Differences and individuality are not allowed. There's an enforced blind obedience to the authority figures of the house.

- **Patterns of codependency and enmeshment.** Since they see others as either saving them or abandoning them, there's a lack of responsibility for them to take care of themselves. They rely on others to always take care of them at the drop of a dime. They see relationships with others as an enmeshment of similar thoughts, opinions, desires, and feelings. There is no interest in or respect for differences.

- **Poor boundaries and difficulty respecting other people's boundaries.** Their self-worth is based on how much they neglect or sacrifice themselves to take care of others and/or how much others neglect or sacrifice themselves for them. Thus, a relationship with an emotionally immature parent feels consuming. It impedes on the time, energy, and interests you have with your other relationships, hobbies, and even career. The parent can have poor boundaries and struggle with saying no, asking for help, and/or respecting when you say no.

What stands out to you as you read through this list? What memories come up? Are there any patterns you notice—any traits that you think may be linked, based on your own childhood experiences? As you move through this workbook, you can return to this list and any notes you took as a reminder of what resonated with you.

Differing Dynamics

It's important to note that every family is unique and there will be different emotional dynamics within families. You might have grown up with two parents who were emotionally immature and in a relationship or one parent who was emotionally immature while the other parent in the relationship was emotionally mature. Maybe you lived with a single parent who was emotionally immature, or you took turns living with separated parents who were both emotionally immature. Maybe you switch off weeks or weekends with an emotionally mature parent and an emotionally immature parent. Or you might've had a stepparent who was emotionally immature. Your own family dynamics will play into what resonates with you in this book as well as the activities you find helpful to your healing.

Childhood Experiences with an Emotionally Immature Parent

As a child, you are affected by the things your parents do and say—and this is no different when you have an emotionally immature parent. In this section, you will learn about the different emotional difficulties and relationship problems that can occur when growing up as the child of an emotionally immature parent. Notice what resonates strongly with you as you continue reading.

Emotional Difficulties

Your relationship with your parent is one of the most important relationships that you have early on in your development. If you didn't have an intimate relationship with your parent and they were unable to show consistent empathy toward you, then you likely experienced a deep emotional loneliness in childhood.

As a child, you couldn't identify the source of this confusing and often painful experience. You simply didn't have the adult knowledge that is necessary to really see things for how they were: toxic and not your fault. Children are egocentric, making sense of the world based on themselves being the center of attention. This isn't inherently bad, but it does make it likely that you internalized your parent's words and behaviors as being your fault. You might've believed that there was something wrong with you and that's why your parent was unhappy, emotionally unavailable, angry, etc. You might've learned that you shouldn't have needs or express your true feelings to your parent because they'd get upset or reject you. Perhaps you learned that you were only a good child when you could make them happy and take care of their needs—that only then were you worthy of their attention, praise, and soothing. This is how a few key emotions, including toxic shame and fear, come into play.

TOXIC SHAME

Toxic shame is the feeling that you are inherently bad, defective, and unworthy of love and belonging. It's often called the master emotion because you can shape your identity around it, losing connection with your true, authentic self and becoming a shame-based person. It's also called the master emotion because you can feel painfully ashamed for experiencing certain emotions, like anger, sadness, excitement, guilt, and fear, or even having certain thoughts, like fantasies, made-up conversations of what you want to say, and wild ideas. Toxic shame can be passed down from generation to generation. Your parent might be a shame-based adult because their parent(s) was/were—and so on up your ancestral line.

FEAR

For many children, there is little as terrifying as not having your parent on your side. Their love, affection, attention, approval, validation, praise, and empathy is what makes you feel safe and like you belong. It makes sense that you would do anything to receive these things from them, even if it meant sacrificing your true, authentic self—your genuine thoughts, feelings, and needs.

It can also feel scary as a child to even consider that your guardian is an emotionally immature adult who might not be capable of providing you with love, safety, and empathy. In your eyes as a child, your parent might've been a god or goddess, king or queen—your ultimate role model who knows everything and rarely, if ever, makes a mistake. It is understandable that you would view them this way; after all, they are your sole means of survival until you become an adult, and most parents will present themselves as knowing more than you—why would you doubt them? Instead, it was likely easier to believe that there was something wrong with you and that's why your parent wasn't loving you, paying attention to you, and caring about you.

This is where the fear of abandonment, rejection, punishment, and not being worthy of love took root for many children of an emotionally immature parent. These fears may have become major motivators in how you acted, what you said, and the confusing and heavy emotions that you experienced as a child. These fears will come up again in the next chapter as you learn more about how the emotional difficulties you had as a child of an emotionally immature parent may have carried over into your adult life.

False Family Roles

The volatile, insecure, and emotionally lonely environment typical of a child of an emotionally immature parent discourages you from developing and connecting with your true, authentic self. Instead, you chase after intimate connection with your parent, who is lacking the capability for empathy and unconditional love.

You might've been trained to conform to rigid expectations or "false family roles" (called "false" because these identities you had to take on are not true to who you really are) in this quest for love and validation. Whether these roles were created in your family out of generational toxic shame or patriarchal norms or other beliefs, they allow predictability so an emotionally immature parent does not have to experience their discomfort surrounding emotional expression.

Certain roles also allow a parent's toxic shame and problems like addictions, abuse, infidelity, punishment, and neglect to continue and remain unaddressed. For example, instead of both parents learning how to navigate through their differences and perhaps seeking marital counseling, their children play peacemaker and caregiver to temporarily "solve" the problem for them—until it repeats itself again and again.

Common false roles children of an emotionally immature parent are taught to play include:

- **High achiever:** Constantly seeks success and validation through accomplishments, often to gain approval or avoid criticism.

- **Hero:** Takes on excessive responsibility and strives for perfection to bring a sense of control and stability to their environment.

- **Sensitive one:** Is highly attuned to the emotions of others and takes on their pain, often at the expense of their own well-being.

- **Caregiver:** Takes on the responsibility of nurturing and supporting others, often at the expense of their own needs and personal growth.

- **Peacemaker:** Tries to maintain harmony in the family by mediating conflicts and suppressing their own emotions.

- **The lost child:** Withdraws and becomes invisible to avoid conflict, seeking solace in solitude and daydreaming.

- **Scapegoat:** Is blamed for the family's problems and dysfunction, often acting out in negative ways to draw attention away from the real issues.

- **Good boy/good girl:** Aims to please others by always following rules, meeting expectations, and avoiding conflict.

- **The mascot:** Uses humor or playfulness to deflect pain and create a sense of relief from family tension.

- **Rebel:** Actively resists authority, challenges norms, and engages in risky behavior as a way to assert independence or deflect attention from deeper issues.

- **Black sheep:** Feels out of place or disconnected from the family, often embracing unconventional or controversial beliefs or behaviors.

- **The angry one:** Frequently displays anger or aggression to cope with underlying emotional pain or frustration.

- **Mom's confidant:** Is closely bonded with their mother, sharing secrets and issues, potentially blurring boundaries and affecting independent relationships.

- **Mom's/Dad's little angel:** Is viewed as perfect and unblemished by a parent, often leading to unrealistic expectations and a fear of failure.

- **Mom's/Dad's best friend:** Forms a close bond with their parent, often serving as a companion, sometimes to the detriment of other relationships or personal development.

Playing these false roles is draining and exhausting because they repress your authentic self. You might not have even been aware of these false masks that you were made to wear, and could still be playing out these old roles now. You will explore more about false roles and self-limiting identities, and how to break free from them, in Part 2.

Growing Up Way Too Soon

As the child of an emotionally immature parent, you might've tried to cope with your emotional loneliness through becoming a little adult—growing up too quickly and too soon. Maybe you became self-sufficient earlier than many of your peers, sacrificed your own needs, and tried to give your parent as little trouble as possible. You might've even wished away childhood, dreaming of finding your freedom and belonging elsewhere through jobs, friendships, and romantic relationships when you grew up.

Even though you might've started acting like a little grownup at a very young age, you were missing the role models in your life to show you important interpersonal skills for engaging in respectful, meaningful, and honest relationships like a mature adult. Also, if you had to skip through your childhood, you might not have had your physical and emotional needs, like attention, encouragement, and support, met; these are needs that only parents or caregivers can provide during the important developmental periods of childhood.

The Wounded Child Inside Your Parent

When it comes to emotionally immature parents, they were once children themselves. Like with you, their emotional difficulties came from somewhere. Likely these difficulties have roots from being raised by their own emotionally immature parent(s) in a home that felt unsafe, unpredictable, and even volatile.

There could've been emotional neglect and even abuse in their homes growing up. Emotional neglect and abuse in any form can be traumatic for a child. These experiences are often lacking the emotional connection, intimacy, support, and safety that are key ingredients for the development of a self-loving, emotionally mature adult. You will learn more about the effects of trauma in the next chapter.

CHAPTER 2

Common Issues Stemming from Being Raised by an Emotionally Immature Parent

The things your parent does and says to you as you are growing up don't just impact that child version of you. They are carried into who you become as an adult. For example, if your parent repeatedly taught you through their actions that you weren't worthy of their love, you can bring this belief of not being worthy into your adulthood, where it affects your adult relationships and how you see yourself in the present. In this chapter, you will learn more about the different ways your emotionally immature parent has contributed to the emotional and relationship challenges you face today. You will reflect on your self-worth and the behavioral patterns of your parent that you may be repeating. An important step toward recovery is seeing where you are now and tracing it back to your experiences with an emotionally immature parent. From here, you will be able to approach healing with the knowledge needed to make the most of this journey.

Emotional Difficulties As an Adult

Do you still feel the constant shame that was a staple in your household while growing up? Are you feeling just as frustrated and unsatisfied with your relationship with your parent today as you did as a child? It is common for the emotional difficulties you experienced in childhood to linger still, especially before you have begun taking intentional steps toward healing. Additionally, new emotional obstacles can crop up as you become an adult.

Toxic Shame

It's normal to feel guilty at times when you say or do something hurtful or wrong; your feelings of guilt help you adjust those behaviors moving forward. However, if you have been taught to feel toxic shame by your emotionally immature parent, you will feel guilty very frequently in adulthood—as if you're always doing something bad or wrong. The shame will be especially strong when you attempt (or even consider) to respect, stand up for, or take care of yourself. This comes from the wound inflicted in childhood of identifying yourself with toxic shame—"I am *bad*. I am unworthy and undeserving of love and belonging." This identity doesn't simply remove itself when you grow up; it is one that you must work to replace over time. Later in this workbook, you will begin healing this wound.

Trauma

You learned a little about trauma in the last chapter. It may have been a part of your own upbringing. If you were exposed to a traumatic event (or multiple traumatic events) as a child, it can have a negative impact on your adult life. It isn't the traumatic events themselves that happened in your childhood that cause long-lasting implications—it's whether or not there was an adult immediately present who supported you, validated your experience, mirrored the intense feelings that were coursing through you, and made you feel safe instead of judged or ashamed as you were going through your intense feelings.

As the child of an emotionally immature parent, it is likely you didn't have the support you deserved in your time of need. As a result, you ended up with unprocessed feelings that remained inside you. These difficult and intense emotions then continue to come up when a present event triggers you. For example, as an adult you may find yourself in an argument in which the other person raises their voice. This brings you back to the trauma of witnessing your parents fight when you were younger. You feel the same emotions and physical sensations you felt at the time of trauma.

These triggers can cause you to have what is known as the fight-flight-freeze-fawn trauma response. You are likely familiar with the fight, flight, and freeze parts of the trauma response. The "fawn" response is a coping mechanism where an individual seeks to appease or accommodate others to avoid conflict, often stemming from a history of trauma or abuse. When you're in a trauma response, you may argue back even louder, manipulate the other person's emotions to feel scared and agree with you through yelling or other aggressive behaviors, run away from the person or avoid them in the future, lose your words and train of thought, or pretend to agree with them just to end the argument.

ARRESTED DEVELOPMENT AND TRAUMA RESPONSES

When a child's needs of receiving empathy and feeling unconditionally loved, safe, and like they belong in their family are not met, they cannot develop properly into a mature adult. This can lead to what is called "arrested development" in which, even though someone is "grown-up," they show signs of immaturity.

In combination with trauma, arrested development can cause a person to revert back to their wounded inner child when they feel triggered. A sign of arrested development is if you find yourself feeling out of control, helpless, terrified, and even as if you are throwing a temper tantrum when having a difficult interaction (especially interactions with your parent). A sign that your parent has arrested development is when it feels and even sounds like you are arguing with a child when you're having a dispute with them.

Arguing with a reactive, emotionally immature adult can feel frustrating and draining, as it often involves dealing with irrational behavior, emotional outbursts, and a lack of empathy or understanding, similar to interacting with a stubborn child. They might say things like, "You're always against me," "It's not fair," "You don't understand me," or "What about me?" Or they may resort to name-calling, diverting the conversation, blame-shifting, using emotionally charged language, and displaying a lack of willingness to engage in constructive dialogue.

A Low Sense of Self

The emotional loneliness and disconnection with your emotions in childhood can create insecurity and anxiety as well as low self-confidence, self-esteem, and self-worth that continue into your adulthood. You were wounded at a deep level. These feelings were repeatedly ingrained in you as the "truth" in your very core. Over time, they have become deep-rooted beliefs that need to be intentionally challenged and removed. They won't simply disappear with age.

Childhood Healing Fantasies

What are childhood healing fantasies? In *Adult Children of Emotionally Immature Parents*, Lindsay C. Gibson, PsyD, describes them as what children naturally create to maintain hope through their emotional, lonely, and painful experiences. These healing fantasies allowed you to imagine that one day in the future you would receive the love, affection, support, and intimacy from your parent that you craved. They were comforting, uplifting fantasies. However, when you carry them into adulthood, they can keep you stuck in the past. The truth is that you cannot make people change, including your parent, no matter how hard you try. You cannot make your parent give you what they are incapable of giving. So, it is necessary to let go of the healing fantasies you created as a child. In this release, you can embrace the reality of your experiences and move closer to healing. You will learn how to let go of your childhood healing fantasies in Part 3.

Emotional Messages

Continued feelings of frustration, dissatisfaction, defeat, anger, and resentment in adulthood are telling you something. They are signals that you're still being disrespected, controlled, ignored, taken advantage of, manipulated, and not truly seen, accepted, validated, or cared for. They are also letting you know that your needs aren't being met. Perhaps you're neglecting your own needs, allowing your parent to over-rely on you, taking too much responsibility for your parent's emotions, or not paying attention to your limits. As unpleasant as they are to experience, these feelings can point you in the direction of healing. Later in this workbook, you will tune into your emotions and use them as a guide in healing.

Adult Relationship Issues

Along with the emotional challenges you may encounter, there are common adult relationship issues that can stem from being raised by an emotionally immature parent. You may notice that many of these issues are also connected to the emotional difficulties explored previously. Emotions, especially how you feel about yourself, are a big part of any relationship, so these challenges are not mutually exclusive.

Chasing What Your Parent Couldn't Give

You may continue to try to relieve your emotional loneliness as an adult by chasing after your parent's attention and love or looking for this validation in other adult relationships. You might also continue playing out false family roles in the hopes of being worthy of what your parent never gave you. However, as you continue looking for self-worth in others, eventually feelings of exhaustion, anger, bitterness, and resentment will arise—toward your parent for neglecting you emotionally and also toward yourself for neglecting who you really are.

Repeating Your Parent's Relationship Dynamics

As an adult, you might notice yourself entering relationships with others who are emotionally immature. It makes sense: This is the dynamic that was modeled to you as a child by your parent. You may even find some comfort in this kind of relationship because it is what you know. In these repeated dynamics, you likely continue to base your self-worth on how good you are at neglecting your own needs and taking care of or rescuing the other person. In turn, the other person may show their emotionally immaturity toward you through the unhealthy patterns explored in Chapter 1.

You might experience emotional loneliness and shame in these relationships, just as you did as a child with your parent. Perhaps you feel guilty when considering your own wants and needs or believe that you are not trying "hard enough" to "deserve" the other person's attention and affection. You may pretend you don't need anything and act as if you don't have any limits or boundaries. You might also struggle with asking for support, what you want, and what you need. Perhaps you assume that the person in your current relationship will reject you for being "needy"—similarly to how your parent responded to your needs. Even if you find yourself in a secure relationship with an emotionally mature person who truly cares about you and is supportive, you'll continue to have the expectation that they aren't interested in your true feelings and will abandon and reject you for having these wants and needs.

As you journey toward recovery, you will be able to break free of these repeated patterns and trust that the people who love and accept you *want* to know how you feel.

Toxic Shame

Continuing to live with toxic shame negatively impacts your adult relationships. Even thinking about asking for help, sharing your true thoughts and feelings, and setting some healthy boundaries will bring up the same childhood fears of being rejected, abandoned, punished, judged, or not worthy of love. Being vulnerable and revealing what's really going on inside exposes the toxic shame that lives within.

However, these feelings of chronic guilt don't mean that you're doing something wrong. You, just like everyone else, deserve to prioritize yourself and express your true thoughts, feelings, and needs. In time, as you move toward healing, you will be able to really internalize this fact.

Lack of Mutual Respect

Respecting someone means you accept who they are and allow them to grow and unfold as they are supposed to, in their own timing, in their own way. In terms of parenting, it's about being more like a caring gardener rather than a carpenter with a blueprint. A gardener provides their seedlings warm and loving sunlight, careful attention, encouragement and praise, and protection from the harsh elements. With this care, they allow their seedling to grow naturally into whatever they are meant to become. A carpenter, on the other hand, has in mind what they want: a picnic table, rocking chair, or maybe a collapsible stool. They will cut, carve, saw, glue, and bend until their materials form into exactly what they want. They get their picnic table, rocking chair, or collapsible stool to use as they please.

Because your emotionally immature parent lacks their own sense of self, individuality, and independence, it is difficult for them to respect you as an adult with your own thoughts and feelings. They might not have received what they needed from their own parent(s) and have now turned to you, using you to get what they want rather than considering your own wants and needs. But that wasn't your responsibility to take on as a child, and it still isn't now as their adult child. Through their self-centeredness, egocentricity, and rigid black-or-white-thinking, they may believe they know what's best for you, at the cost of respecting the choices that you make.

If you are being disrespected by your parent or by other adults, it will create emotional distress, bringing up feelings like anger, resentment, and frustration. This in turn creates tension, strain, and distance in the relationship. If respect is missing within a relationship, it will eat away your trust in yourself and that other person. Also, persistent disrespect from your parent or by other adults can result in a diminished sense of self-worth and self-esteem.

The Inner Critic

Words are powerful; they are spells, manifesting the reality you live in. Unfortunately there tends to be an inner critic in us all. An often overlooked relationship that lives in our minds, this critic speaks in the form of negative self-talk. It may point out your insecurities. Or perhaps it discounts your strengths and achievements as "luck" or just a "coincidence." If you were raised by an emotionally immature parent, it may repeat the worst things they said to you as a child. Even though you might've physically left home, your inner critic allows the hurtful voice of your parent to continue replaying in your mind. You might've also repeated the same words of your parent to yourself out loud or tolerated other people saying similar things.

As part of healing, it's important to begin observing your inner critic. Self-awareness will be your first step in replacing this inner critic with the compassionate self-love that empowers you and eases past wounds. You will learn more about developing self-awareness in the next chapter. Then in Chapter 6, you will practice shifting your inner voice to one of encouragement and love. Recovery awaits.

CHAPTER 3

Preparing to Heal

Now that you have learned more about emotional immaturity and how your emotions and relationships have been impacted by an emotionally immature parent, it's time to prepare for healing. This chapter will explore the tools that will be important to your recovery. You will discover why boundaries are key to healthy relationships and reflect on where boundaries may be lacking in your own life. Then you will learn about the power of self-awareness. Here, you will find mindfulness practices, like meditation and written reflection, that will come up again and again in Parts 2 and 3 of this workbook. You will also try a beginner meditation to set things in motion for Part 2. Let's start the journey to healing.

The Importance of Boundaries

Boundaries are an act of self-care, self-love, self-respect, self-advocacy, and self-protection. They are also important building blocks of healthy, sustainable relationships. Without clear and firm boundaries, you can feel emotionally drained, used, or unseen. Relationships that don't have boundaries become codependent and emotionally enmeshed, meaning:

- They feel one-sided.

- There is enabling of harmful behaviors, as these issues are minimized, excused, ignored, or denied.

- There is either direct or indirect controlling behavior, for example, telling the other person what to do or judging, guilt-tripping, or "shoulding" ("You should have done this," "You shouldn't do that") each other.

- You over-rely on the other person to meet your needs instead of trying to meet them yourself.

- You feel uncomfortable being yourself and accepting them for who they are.

- You confuse supporting someone with rescuing, fixing, and improving them.

- You take responsibility for someone else's happiness.

- Genuine thoughts and feelings aren't expressed by one or both of you due to worry, guilt, and fear.

- You absorb the other person's emotions while ignoring your own.

- You give control of your life to the other person.

- You're uncomfortable being alone and can't enjoy time alone.

- You don't know who you are, and you don't have a sense of your own identity outside of the relationship.

- You are emotionally dependent: If they feel happy, you feel happy; if they feel upset, you feel upset.

- You need validation and approval from the other person in order to make decisions.

- You feel bad if you prioritize yourself.

- You confuse the quantity of time spent with someone with the quality of time spent.

- When the other person is upset or angry with you, you can't stop thinking about it, you feel very guilty and blame yourself, and you immediately try to fix the problem.

The presence of some or many of these elements reflect a codependent and/or enmeshed relationship.

Emotionally Immature Parents and a Lack of Boundaries

These patterns of codependency and enmeshment can start very early on, in your early relationship with your emotionally immature parent. Your parent may not have had healthy boundaries themselves, so they couldn't model healthy relationships with clear and firm boundaries to you.

Not only could they not teach you about or model healthy boundaries (they likely didn't know what they were), but there very likely were frequent boundary violations throughout your younger years. A common physical boundary violation is forcing you to hug to relatives, family friends, and even strangers. Another physical boundary violation common in some cultures is talking about someone's weight. Growing up as a child of emotionally immature parents in an Asian culture, I often heard things like, "Are you eating? You've lost weight. So skinny" or "Wow. You've gained weight—especially on your cheeks!"

In Part 3, you will learn more about the different types of boundaries that may have been violated in your past experiences.

Signs That You Need to Start Setting Boundaries

Warning signs will begin to appear in your mind, body, and emotions when you aren't living a life that's true to you, taking care of and respecting yourself, and setting necessary boundaries and limits within your relationship with your parent (and others). Here are some signs that you are in need of some healthy, firm boundaries:

- You feel overwhelmed, exhausted, and nearing (or already experiencing) burnout.

- You feel resentful in your relationships—it's not fair how you're being treated, and it's not fair that other people don't have to deal with what you're dealing with.

- You avoid people, interactions, phone calls, and texts just in case they might ask you for something or to avoid a nonreciprocal conversation with the other person.

- You create time out of thin air for everyone else, even strangers, but you don't make any time for yourself.

- You say yes most or all the time even when you want or need to say no, then you'll either lie to try to get out of what you said yes to or do it grudgingly.

- You daydream about escaping everything and everyone—all your obligations and responsibilities—very often.

- You don't really know who you are when you're alone or separated from your relationship; you don't know what you need or want.

- You allow others to over-rely on you and/or you over-rely on others.

- You tolerate repeating relationship issues without saying anything—even though these issues make you feel hurt, angry, disrespected, taken advantage of, manipulated, uncomfortable, scared, unseen, unheard, bullied, dismissed, and/or controlled.

The more of these signs that you experience, the more likely it is that you are lacking healthy boundaries within your relationships. As you go through the list, circle or check off the signs that resonate with you to shed light on whether you are lacking healthy boundaries.

Establishing and maintaining firm, healthy boundaries with your emotionally immature parent is crucial to your independence and freedom. It's also going to be one of the most difficult relationships to set these boundaries in—especially if you haven't already started. This is normal: It's one of the relationships where you have the most history. Your parent has known you longer than anyone; they've been seeing you, treating you, and talking to you in certain patterns, whether unintentionally or intentionally. When it comes to their relationship with you, they are used to being controlling, defensive, passive-aggressive, etc.

Though it can feel uncomfortable or even scary at first, having healthy boundaries with your parent will teach them how to treat you, talk to you with respect, and best show up for you. You're going to be approaching a very old relationship in a new way. There will naturally be resistance and turbulence at the start—you will be *rocking the ship*—as you and your parent go through the growing pains of setting and sticking to boundaries. However, it is so worth this effort, and you will find life changed for the better. In Part 3, you will discover just how to set healthy boundaries as well as how to maintain them when your parent pushes back.

Exploring Your Inner World

In addition to setting healthy boundaries, looking within will be key in creating healthier relationships with your parent, yourself, and others. After all, inner changes and growth cannot occur if you're not aware of what's going on inside of you. By looking within, you can observe your emotionally immature parent more objectively and clearly. This self-awareness will help you let go of childhood healing fantasies while healing your childhood wounds, release your toxic shame and false family roles, regulate your emotions, and navigate through your triggers and habitual reactions in relationships. Most importantly, this new awareness will allow you to rediscover your true, authentic self.

The activities in Chapter 4 will take you through the practice of exploring your inner world, but it is helpful to first have a foundational understanding of the different methods for self-awareness. This knowledge will allow you to make the most of the activities not only in Chapter 4 but also throughout Parts 2 and 3 of this book. You will notice these methods being used again and again across different themes and practices.

Meditation

One amazing way to explore your inner world is through the practice of meditation. Meditation has numerous mental health and well-being benefits that include reducing stress and anxiety, improving emotional regulation, enhancing focus and concentration, boosting mood and well-being, and improving physical health. Overall, a regular meditation practice can be a powerful tool to improve your mental, emotional, and physical health, and develop greater self-awareness, resilience, and well-being. Once you have developed your meditation practice, you can essentially practice it anywhere, anytime, no matter what is going on around or within you.

A QUICK GUIDE TO MEDITATION FOR BEGINNERS

If meditation is new to you or you tried it before but quit because your mind was too distracted or it felt boring or uncomfortable, this guide is for you. Yes, it can initially be challenging to meditate, but just like anything else, it gets easier with practice. And actually, meditation is not about stopping thinking, getting rid of thoughts, or having the *perfect* focus so that you never get distracted. I've been meditating regularly for a decade and still experience lots of thoughts and wander off in my stream of thoughts during meditation. It's my *relationship* with my thoughts that has changed. I don't get lost in thought for as long as I did when starting out, and I am able to observe my thoughts and feelings with less judgment and criticism.

A helpful way to approach both meditation and the exploration of your inner world is with COLOR:

- **Curiosity.** Be curious of what you notice.

- **Open-mindedness.** Be open to whatever thoughts, feelings, and sensations arrive moment by moment.

- **Lightness.** The practice does take some applied effort and discipline, but don't take yourself or the practice too seriously; encourage some lightness and gentleness in your practice.

- **Openheartedness.** Practice with an open heart, meeting yourself and the uncomfortable, sad, angry, bitter, and even terrifying inner experiences with love.

- **Receptiveness.** Don't judge what comes up as good or bad. Accept and allow whatever shows up to be there.

You will find guided meditation practices to supplement and deepen some of the workbook activities throughout Part 2 and Part 3. You may follow these exactly or alter certain steps according to what feels right for you. Or you may choose to skip the guided meditation and follow the instructions that are provided in the activity itself. It is entirely your choice.

Written Reflection and Journaling

Written reflection and journaling can be incredibly beneficial for mental health and personal growth. This practice can increase self-awareness, improve emotional regulation, enhance creativity, provide greater clarity and focus, and build your problem-solving skills. Through self-reflection and journaling, you can learn from your past and continually improve.

Therapy

Therapy is another helpful tool for tuning in to your inner world and developing greater self-awareness. Through therapy, you can explore your inner world with a trusted professional who can offer you more objectivity and helpful tools for understanding yourself and your experiences. Therapy can also help you to develop greater empathy and understanding of others and to improve your relationships with loved ones.

Mindful Movement

Mindful movement practices, like yoga, tai chi, dance, or qigong, can be an effective way to develop self-awareness and improve physical and mental health. These practices involve a combination of movement and breath work to help you ground yourself in the present and sift through racing thoughts and feelings with more clarity and calm. Meditation will often be woven into mindful movement for an even more effective self-awareness practice.

Connecting with Nature

Spending time in nature can be an effective way to develop self-awareness. By observing and connecting with the natural world, you can become more grounded in the present, calm yourself, and filter out the racing thoughts and feelings that are clouding your mind and body.

PART 2

ACTIVITIES FOR ACCEPTING THE REALITIES OF EMOTIONALLY IMMATURE PARENTS

Now that you have laid the groundwork for healing, it's time to begin. In this part, you will tune into the world within. You will be discovering (or rediscovering) who you really are as you practice self-reflection and self-awareness. There are also guided meditations that you can integrate to experience the lessons at an even deeper level. Through the activities in this part, you will find a greater understanding and clarity of not only yourself but also your emotionally immature parent and your relationship with them—and others. This inner work will prepare you for Part 3, where you will be applying what you've learned in your relationships in order to move forward with healthier bonds.

Go slowly, be gentle with yourself, and take breaks as you go through these activities. Share your insights and practices with trusted friends and loved ones as you go along. You can even work through some of the exercises with a loved one to strengthen your connection right then. This part is designed for you to go through the activities in order. However, once you've made it through all the exercises, you can revisit different ones that call to you. And the guided meditations are for you to practice as often as you desire. You'll be learning, growing, changing, and healing with every effort you make, so you might discover something new each time you revisit activities.

CHAPTER 4

Finding Home Within

Unlocking Self-Awareness

Home is not just a place where you rest your head at night. It is also a place inside of you where you exist as your truest self. In this chapter, you'll learn how to become more aware of this inner world through practicing mindfulness. You will develop your skills of self-reflection to help you understand yourself, learn from past mistakes, and recognize adjustments that are needed for a more positive relationship with your parent. With this greater self-awareness, you will be ready to navigate the difficult emotions in Chapter 5 and continue bringing mindfulness to the rest of this workbook (and your daily life). It's time to befriend your mind, becoming less judging and critical toward yourself and creating more inner peace.

Discovering You

VENTURING WITHIN

ONE OF THE MOST IMPORTANT relationships that you will ever have is the one that you have with yourself. After all, you spend every single day with yourself. Do you have a loving, encouraging, and kind relationship with yourself, or is it judgmental, discouraging, and mean? If your emotional needs, like affection and validation, were neglected, ignored, and/or dismissed in your experiences growing up with an emotionally immature parent, you may continue to discount your own needs (or you may even not be able to recognize that your needs are being unmet) in your adult life with your parent and other adult relationships. To start treating yourself with the care that you deserve, you must first explore who you really are.

Here's HOW You get to know someone deeply by spending time with them, doing things with them that they enjoy, and being kind and empathetic toward them. It's time to get to know yourself in the same way.

Put It Into PRACTICE Every day moving forward, block out small chunks of time (5–20 minutes) to spend with yourself. Make this your sacred time with no distractions by hiding your cell phone and prioritizing this time over your parent's needs or worrying about your parent. During this time, you can do one or more of the following:

1. Meditate inwardly, becoming sensitive and aware of what thoughts, feelings, memories, and bodily sensations show up in your mind and body.

2. Give yourself permission to do things that you enjoy.

3. Complete activities in this workbook.

As you spend this quality time with yourself, reflect on what thoughts and feelings come up and what insight you receive into yourself. Record your reflection so you can revisit it and add to it:

There is no one else who could know you as deeply as you could know yourself. It'll be crucial to your healing and growth for you to continue directing your focus and attention to learning about yourself.

Remember:

● It's never too late to discover who you really are.

● The relationship that you have with yourself is one of the most important relationships that you will ever have.

● Self-awareness through directing your attention inward and spending quality time with yourself is how you can discover your individuality and independent sense of self.

2 Noticing Your Thoughts

THOUGHTS ARE LIKE IMAGE FRAMES that make up a captivating movie on the big screen. The frames move so quickly in your mind's eye, one after another, and seem so vivid and alive that it's easy to get absorbed into them. Fortunately, developing a more objective awareness of your thoughts will shine a light on negative reactive thoughts and initial emotional reactions that are triggered by your parent. This awareness will give you the option to *respond* rather than *react*.

Here's HOW This is where mindfulness comes in. By practicing mindfulness, you can train your mind to be more present and aware of both your outer surroundings and your inner world of thoughts and feelings so you're observing them through a more objective, rational lens. You will be like a patron who remembers they're watching a film in a movie theater and thus can create some emotional distance rather than getting completely absorbed and forgetting that thoughts and feelings are not an accurate portrayal of your real life.

Put It Into PRACTICE In this simple exercise you're going to train yourself to be in the present through your six senses of seeing, touching, hearing, smelling, tasting, and thinking. Follow these steps:

1. Notice five distinct shapes in your surroundings and draw them.

2. Notice four distinct colors in your area and describe them.

_____

_____

_____

3. Notice and touch three different textures around you and describe them.

_____

_____

_____

4. Notice one sound immediately near you and one sound that's farther away. Where are they coming from?

_____

_____

_____

5. Notice one smell around you, whether it's in the air or on yourself. What is it?

_____

_____

_____

6. Notice something that you can taste; if there's a snack nearby, give it a lick or a bite, or if there are no food items around, give yourself a lick. What do you taste?

_____

_____

_____

7. Lastly, notice what thought just popped up into your mind. Perhaps it's simply something like, *Wait. What thought?* Write it down.

If you feel calmer and more ready, you may now revisit your thoughts about your emotionally immature parent and try to look at it. These thoughts may come in the form of a memory of an emotionally charged exchange that you had with them. See if you can revisit this memory of a difficult experience involving you and your parent through a lens of kindness and compassion for yourself and what happened. And if you want a challenge, see if you can extend kindness and compassion toward your parent as well. Or you may put it out of mind for now and embrace your calm, renewed, and present mindset.

Remember:

- The first step to change, growth, and healing is self-awareness.

- Mindfulness means being present and paying attention with purpose and a nonjudgmental attitude.

- Thoughts are very vivid and lifelike, but they're not always true and you don't have to live them.

3 Building on Your Mindfulness Skills

A GUIDED MEDITATION FOR ABSOLUTE BEGINNERS

Without self-awareness it is difficult for an emotionally imma-ture parent to notice the thoughts and feelings that they are experiencing. Rather than being able to respond to their inner world, they are reactive. It is likely that they taught you this reactivity as well, and it will take time and practice to undo this teaching. This is why this workbook provides different activities for regularly stretching your mindfulness muscle.

One way you can become more mindful of your own inner world is through having a regular meditation practice. Mindfulness meditation is a simple yet profound practice that can literally rewire your brain as you become more present, centered, calm, and in control. Becoming more mindful will help you not only see and make changes to the relationship that you have with your mind but also identify when you're encountering situations that bring up uncomfortable thoughts and feelings. By recogniz-ing these moments, you will be better prepared to face the discomfort. You will be more equipped to set boundaries and express your true feelings with your parent and others.

Here's HOW Training your mind to become more mindful will challenge the brain's natural laziness in doing the least amount of work possible. It'll require you to pay attention to whatever stimulations and sensations that are currently here all around you and inside of you. You can pay attention to whatever you're doing with mindfulness—moment by moment nonjudgmental presence—whether you're doing a mundane task or entering a heated argument with your parent. This mindfulness medi-tation training starts with paying attention to your moving breath.

Put It Into PRACTICE If you are new to meditation, you can practice with the guided meditation at EmotionallyImmatureParents .com This meditation will set the stage for the later meditations that are specific to your experiences with an emotionally immature parent. If you do not wish to use the guided meditation, you can follow these steps:

1. Set a timer for 1–5 minutes. (Decide on an amount of time that you can be consistent with and ideally be able to practice daily. Doing less time consistently is better than more time inconsistently.)

2. Sit or lay down in a comfortable position.

3. Begin tuning in to your sensations (sounds, temperature, texture of your clothing, smell, etc.).

4. Now bring the spotlight of your attention to your breathing (at the top of the nose, chest, or belly).

5. Maintain your awareness in the present moment by observing each and every passing breath.

6. If the spotlight of your attention wanders off into thoughts (memories, fantasies, future worries, made-up conversations, etc.), just bring it back to your breath.

7. Repeat steps 4 to 6 until the timer runs out.

Here are some follow-up questions that you can ask yourself after each meditation practice:

1. How do my emotions, body, and mind feel now as compared to before the meditation?

2. What thoughts did my attention wander into? Was there a specific memory or a future event or made-up scenario that my mind kept wandering into? How did it make me feel engaging in these thoughts?

Compare your answers to these questions over time as you gain more practice in meditation.

Remember:

- Mindfulness means paying attention in an intentional way without self-judgment.

- Mindfulness can be practiced throughout the day, whether you are doing a chore or having a difficult conversation.

- You can continue to strengthen your skills in mindfulness by practicing meditation regularly and seeing how you develop.

4 Releasing Judgment

BREAKING FREE OF HURTFUL CRITIQUE

BEING RAISED BY AN EMOTIONALLY immature parent who was critical, judgmental, harsh, and shame-based, you may have been constantly judged based on strict standards. And these standards also might have been constantly changing depending on your parent's mood. So starting at a very young age, you began to judge and criticize yourself—and others too. Judging is a powerful human ability, but when it goes past the point of giving us useful information to make a decision, it can become harmful. Whatever you judge positively, you will crave, resist losing, and feel sad when you do lose it. Whatever you judge negatively, you will avoid, push away, and feel bad when it's present. It's time for a new perspective.

Here's HOW You can find much more happiness, lightness, and freedom with yourself and within your relationships when you let go of the tendency toward judgmental thoughts. Start noticing when you are judging yourself, other people, and interactions, and challenge those judgments.

Put It Into PRACTICE The next time you become aware of a judgmental and critical thought, label it as "judging." Now ask yourself these questions to begin shifting your perspective:

1. What am I judging about this? What critical thoughts come up?

2. What's another perspective to see this situation/person from? Ask yourself, "What might be happening in their life for them to behave this way?"

_____

_____

3. What if I didn't judge this situation/person? How would I think differently about it/them? How would I feel differently about it/them?

_____

_____

4. If you were judging yourself negatively, ask yourself what will you do differently the next time? What will you do similarly?

_____

_____

You'll find that the judgment runs deep. It will take time and consistent effort to change your thoughts from being critical to more open-minded. As you practice this activity, you'll find that you'll be gentler on yourself and with your parent and that you can still make positive changes in your life without all the judgment.

Remember:

- There's nothing wrong with judging when it offers us useful information and it helps us make accurate decisions.

- Judging becomes a problem when you constantly judge things and people in unconstructive ways.

- You can choose to learn from past experiences and mistakes, make appropriate adjustments, and try again without beating yourself and others up again and again.

5 Clearing a Space in the Dense Forest of Your Mind

A GUIDED MEDITATION FOR INNER PEACE

THE QUALITY OF YOUR HOMELIFE growing up and the family dynamics that existed impacts the quality of your mind, your personal relationship with yourself, and the quality of your relationships as an adult. If you didn't feel safe at home, like you were always walking on eggshells, and it was unpredictable how your parent may react, you may have a high-alert, anxious, worrying, and hypervigilant mind. If you had to take care of your parent's needs and their wants while you were growing up, you may constantly attend to others while neglecting your own needs. Or you might've rushed to become more "mature" and hyperindependent with little to no maintenance. You need to direct your energy—your attention, focus, and time—inwardly if you're to find peace within as an adult.

Here's HOW Finding this inner peace isn't about creating something out of nothing or getting rid of the "anxious" parts of your mind and only focusing on positive and calming thoughts. It's about making a clearing in the chaos—the dense forest—of your mind.

Put It Into PRACTICE In this practice, you will cultivate inner peace by using a tree visualization in the guided meditation provided at EmotionallyImmatureParents.com. If you don't want to practice the guided meditation or don't have access to the website, think of a space that has made you feel safe in the past. What was it about this time and place that made you feel safe? Were you alone? Was someone else with you? What details do you remember about this place? Note the feelings inside your body. Then place one hand to your heart center and the other hand to your belly.

Imagine you are the trunk of a great, ancient tree, both grounded and tall. Just be with the safe memory, the feeling of being grounded and tall, and whatever sensations that are present for at least 30 seconds.

Breathe deeply into the trunk of the tree as whatever sensations, thoughts, and feelings arrive and disappear. You are strong, firm, and yet yielding. You are in your inner safe space. Revisit it as often as possible.

Once you find your inner safe space, you'll realize how precious it is. You will become more empowered to stop external situations from taking your inner peace away from you.

Write down your observations.

Remember:

- There lives a vast and complex world inside of you, and that's where you'll discover your inner peace.

- Getting comfortable with being quiet and still as well as dwelling in silence are necessary to creating a clearing in the dense, busy forest of your mind.

- Your inner peace can be visited whenever you need some calm or clarity.

6 Becoming a Kind and Curious Detective

A SELF-REFLECTION

A TRAIT OF EMOTIONAL IMMATURITY is lacking self-reflection. Without practicing self-reflection, it makes it difficult for your parent to recognize what their part is in relationship issues and how their actions impact you.

On your own path to self-reflection, it's important to differentiate reflection with rumination and overthinking. Growing up with an emotionally immature parent, you might have learned that it's terrible to make mistakes. The fear and shame that are linked with making mistakes can lead you to fixate on, replay, and overanalyze past mistakes in a way that's not helpful. Ruminating over the past can bring up negative emotions, like guilt, shame, anger, resentment, regret, and bitterness. While practicing self-reflection may bring up uncomfortable feelings, you are learning from your past experiences and mistakes in a productive way so you can make changes moving forward.

Here's HOW You can practice productive self-reflection through a short, daily practice of journaling. You may journal about your day, an event, an interaction, a memory, etc.—writing whatever's in your mind. It's a good idea to revisit past journal entries as well because there is so much wisdom inside of you, and sometimes you will rediscover valuable insights that you had in the past.

Put It Into PRACTICE The intention here is to practice a growth-oriented mindset by learning from your past mistakes and changing your perspective so it is more accurate rather than distorted from faulty ways of thinking. If you find yourself feeling bad or guilty as you go through this activity, remind yourself, "I'm learning as I go. It's normal to make mistakes. I know better now so I'll try better now."

Reflect on a past negative interaction that you had with one or both of your parents:

1. What happened? Who was there? Where were you?

_____

_____

_____

_____

2. What did you feel during the interaction? What did you feel after? What are you feeling now when thinking about the interaction?

_____

_____

_____

_____

3. What went well in the interaction? What went poorly?

_____

_____

_____

_____

4. Did you do or say something you wish you hadn't? Did you not do or say something that you wished you had?

_____

_____

_____

_____

5. Did they do or say something you wish they hadn't? Did they not do or say something that you wish they had?

_____

_____

_____

_____

_____

_____

6. Next time, how would you navigate through this kind of situation differently?

_____

_____

_____

_____

_____

_____

Remember:

- Your emotionally immature parent may be lacking the ability to self-reflect.

- Practicing self-reflection allows you to learn from your past, understand how your inner world impacts your outer world, and identify new courses of action to take in the future.

- Self-reflection is different from ruminating and overanalyzing a past memory. They both involve the past, but self-reflection is growth-oriented, while ruminating and overanalyzing is punishment-oriented.

7 Understanding the Power of Questions

SELF-DISCOVERY THROUGH SELF-INQUIRY

EVEN THOUGH YOUR PARENT MAY have been around physically and participated in the stereotypical family events, like birthday dinners, graduations, etc., they may have still been absent in other ways. You may not have experienced an emotional connection, encouraging support, and empathy: the things that make a parent feel like a safe haven that you *know* you can turn to no matter what and no matter when. Without this haven, there was a lack of the safety and encouragement needed for you to really explore and enjoy who you are. Luckily, it's never too late to discover who you are. Along with spending quality time with yourself in Activity 1: Discovering You, you can continue to get to know yourself even more deeply through self-inquiry.

Here's HOW Rather than turning to external validations, approval, and answers from your parent, you can build a habit of asking yourself the things you might ask other people. Instead of asking your parent what they need, how about asking yourself what you need? Instead of just focusing on what someone else might want to do, why not consider what you want? It's okay if answers don't show up right away. It's okay to feel confused, numb, and frustrated because you don't know *yet* what your answers are. Just keep asking and knocking on that door to your inner world every day, and someday soon your answers will meet you at the door and let you in.

Put It Into PRACTICE Here are simple questions to explore your inner world:

1. What do I need right now? Is there anything that feels missing?

2. What do I want right now?

3. How am I feeling right now?

4. What's important to me? What are my top three values?

5. If I took a chance on myself, what new hobbies, interests, opportunities, or career paths would I want to try out?

6. What does my ideal day look like? Where am I? Who is there? What am I doing? Wearing? Eating?

7. What do I like? What makes me happy?

8. What do I dislike? What's something that I care very little about?

Remember:

- Growing up with an emotionally immature parent, you may have been taught to focus your energy externally, finding answers and validation from others. Part of healing will be unlearning this.

- You can open the door to your inner world by asking yourself questions.

- You have the answers that you are looking for inside of you—you just need to be patient in continuing to ask—and listen.

8 Tuning In to Your Senses

BECOMING MORE SELF-AWARE EVERY DAY

MINDFUL MEDITATION DOESN'T HAVE TO be reserved for longer blocks of time where you stop what you are doing, sit or lie down, close your eyes, and do a full meditation. It can happen at any time of the day, when you are doing any activity—even when you are sleeping.

In meditation, you learn to have your moving breath as the focus of your attention. To bring this mindfulness into each aspect of your day, you must carry the same intentional energy—paying attention moment by moment without judging—to whatever that you are doing. Continuing to develop self-awareness with daily mindfulness will help you get to know yourself more, be able to see your parent more objectively without getting as emotionally hooked and reactive, give you more space and time to respond rather than react to unexpected situations, and help you with regulating your emotions.

Here's HOW The sensations that land upon your six sense doors (sight, sound, smell, taste, body sensation, and thoughts) provide the perfect way to capture your attention. You can become more mindful and in the moment by noticing facial expressions, the volume and tone of voices, the beating of your heart, any tension in your body, how the room you are in smells and looks, what clothes other people are wearing, etc. From heated conversations to mundane tasks, any situation is an opportunity to be mindful.

Put It Into
PRACTICE

1. Practice mindfulness while doing a mundane task. Maybe you go for a walk, clean your room, or wash your dishes. Try to be as present as possible during this task and notice the details of it with your six senses. For example, if you decide to go wash some dishes, notice the sound of the scrubbing, the weight of each dish, the sound of draining water, the texture of the soap, the passing thought about what you want to do next, etc.

2. Once you've completed the mundane task, write what you experienced as if you're sharing with someone who has never done such a task before:

_____

_____

_____

_____

_____

_____

_____

_____

_____

_____

Remember:

- You can practice mindfulness with whatever task you're doing.

- The six senses of taste, touch, smell, sound, sight, and thought are the perfect tools for focusing on the present.

- Through this regular practice, you are developing your knowledge of who you are as well as your abilities to respond rather than react and to regulate your emotions.

CHAPTER 5

Learning What Your Parent Couldn't Show You

The Language of Feelings

As the child of an emotionally immature parent, you may have little experience in recognizing or processing different emotions. It's never too late to cultivate these skills. In this chapter, you'll level up your emotional intelligence by learning how to recognize, name, assess, and manage your feelings. You'll also level up your emotional resilience by building a greater capacity to be with and navigate through emotional situations. Then you'll discover a tool to help regulate your emotions. And later in the chapter, you will learn how to begin putting your feelings into words, preparing yourself to express your feelings in Part 3. You'll also practice being more supportive and encouraging toward yourself as you take care of your emotional needs.

9   Feeling All the Feels

WHAT YOUR BODY CAN TELL YOU

THERE IS A DIFFERENCE BETWEEN thinking and feeling: Thinking is the language of the mind, and feeling is the language of the body. Your parent might have been lacking emotional intelligence and sensitivity, so they were unable to teach and model to you how to feel your feelings.

When an adult doesn't know how to feel or process their emotions, it can lead to various mental and emotional issues, like anxiety, depression, emotional numbness, low self-esteem, poor coping habits, or chronic stress. It can also lead to relationship difficulties, like ineffective communication, lack of emotional intimacy, misunderstandings, arguments, and conflicts.

Each of your emotions sparks a unique cocktail of chemicals and hormones that floods your body. Think of your body as a helpful messenger showing you that you are experiencing emotion.

Here's HOW   To start feeling your feelings, just tune into these messages from your body. Where do they show up? Common places where your feelings can come up in your body include your face, jaw, neck, shoulders, chest, belly, and hips.

Put It Into PRACTICE   Close your eyes and tune into your body. Notice whatever feelings are present. You will expand your emotional vocabulary in the next activity to better understand what you're feeling, but for now simply start noticing these emotions:

1. Where in your body are you experiencing a feeling (clenched jaw, shrugging up of the shoulders, queasiness in the stomach)?

2. What emotion might be connected to this sensation? For example, anxiety can be found in clenching the jaw or experiencing back pain. If you can't name the emotion, how would you describe it to someone?

3. What color would this emotion be? Bright red? Murky brown?

4. What shape would this emotion be? Round? Sharp? Blurry?

5. What texture would this emotion be? Smooth? Rough?

6. Lastly, draw out what this feeling looks like to you.

Your feelings are just as important as your thoughts. They provide you with valuable information about what you are experiencing. Please be gentle, patient, and kind with yourself as you practice noticing the feelings that come up and describing them.

Remember:

- Your feelings are the language of your body, while your thoughts are the language of your mind. Both languages are important.

- Body sensations are helpful signals of emotions that need to be felt right now.

- Be patient as you practice feeling your feelings. More understanding will come later and with effort.

10 | Leveling Up Emotionally, Part 1
EMOTIONAL INTELLIGENCE

YOUR EMOTIONALLY IMMATURE PARENT MIGHT'VE truly tried their best, but they had limited emotional intelligence (the ability to assess, monitor, and manage emotions). They may have been unable to teach you and show you how to feel your feelings as they lacked that skill themselves. Instead, you might've been punished, shamed, ignored, or abandoned by your parent when you were feeling certain things like anger and sadness.

The ability to feel is important: It gives you valuable information about your inner world as well as your surroundings. Sometimes you can get even more accurate information about situations and other people than your logical brain can compute. Feelings are what give life meaning, and this is why your next step in recovery will be leveling up your own emotional intelligence.

Here's HOW You can level up your emotional intelligence by first learning the names of different feelings. If you can't name it, it makes it difficult for you to be able to monitor and regulate your emotions—let alone talk about or express them. In this activity, you will expand your emotional vocabulary with the help of an "emotional wheel."

Put It Into PRACTICE

1. Search images for "emotional wheel" and find one that you like. There are many different emotional wheels available, but they typically share a similar structure: a three-layered wheel with the core emotions in the center.

2. Ask yourself, "How am I feeling right now?"

3. Starting from the center of the wheel, try your best to identify which core emotion you are experiencing right now. Not completely sure? A guess is perfectly fine.

4. Move on to the second layer of the wheel. Depending on the core emotion you're feeling, select from the list what emotions are within your core emotion.

5. Move on to the third layer of the wheel. Which emotions resonate on this layer?

6. Using what you discovered in the previous steps, how are you feeling right now?

_____

_____

_____

_____

_____

_____

7. Of course, you may notice that you're feeling more than one core emotion at a time: You can go through the emotional wheel again and again to identify all the emotions that you're feeling right now. Try checking in with your emotions throughout the day; go through the emotional wheel to name how you're feeling.

Remember:

● Emotional intelligence is the ability to assess, monitor, and manage your emotions and other people's emotions.

● Using an emotional wheel will help you level up your emotional intelligence.

● You can experience many emotions at one time.

11 Understanding the Full Spectrum of Emotions
THE POTENTIAL IN EVERY FEELING

YOUR EMOTIONALLY IMMATURE PARENT MIGHT'VE been very uncomfortable and ashamed with their feelings and in turn may have shamed or tried to prevent you from experiencing certain feelings. The common emotions that you may have learned to feel ashamed about and even dislike include guilt, anger, anxiety, excitement, and sadness. But wait: Don't kill the messenger.

There's no such thing as "good" or "bad" emotions. They can all be insightful. Guilt often lets you know when you did something unethical or against your values so you can adjust your behaviors. Anger can signal if you're in danger, being taken advantage of, disrespected, or manipulated. Anxiety often lets you know what's important to you. Some anxiety, similar to excitement, can even boost your performance. Sadness lets you know that you care about something or someone and that you are experiencing loss. Feeling sadness allows you to process the loss and move on.

Here's HOW In order to seize the true potential of your emotions, you'll have to unlearn that there are good feelings (ones that you want to have) and bad feelings (ones that you don't want to have) and learn to welcome, feel, and learn from all of them.

Put It Into PRACTICE Imagine that you're a welcoming guesthouse and your emotions are like unexpected visitors that show up and need a place to stay. (This activity is inspired from Rumi's poem "The Guest House"; you can find more information on this in the Additional Book Resources section.)

1. What emotions are you comfortable with that you want to keep forever and never let leave your guesthouse?

2. What emotions are you uncomfortable with that you don't want to let inside your guesthouse?

3. What is it about the emotions in your second answer that you don't like? When do they show up? What situations and/or relationships trigger them?

4. What might these emotions be trying to tell you? About yourself? About the situation?

5. What might these emotions be trying to tell you about the other person/relationship?

With this insight, set the intention to welcome your emotions moving forward. Allow them to stay in your guesthouse until they are ready to leave.

Remember:

- Emotions clue you into something important.

- Treat your emotions like visitors. No matter who they are, no matter what the emotion is, welcome and entertain them all.

- Your emotions will leave on their own once you've let them in, processed them, listened to them, and learned from them.

12 Leveling Up Emotionally, Part 2

A GUIDED MEDITATION IN EMOTIONAL RESILIENCE

EMOTIONAL RESILIENCE IS YOUR ABILITY to stay calm and focused among the challenges of life. It is like a muscle, getting stronger the more that you face emotional situations, like setting boundaries with your parent. With experience, you become more familiar with, and even used to, the uncomfortable feelings, thoughts, and sensations that arise in these challenging situations. Rather than avoiding, running away, or shutting down from challenges, cultivating emotional resilience enables you to face issues head-on.

Here's HOW In this activity, you will build emotional resilience by facing a challenging situation and taking steps to navigate it calmly. Before getting started, think of a future challenging situation or event that you want the emotional resilience to tackle (e.g., setting a boundary with your mom). If nothing comes to mind, think about a past challenge that you wish you had more resilience when handling (e.g., having a difficult conversation with your dad).

Put It Into PRACTICE Follow the guided meditation provided at Emotionally ImmatureParents.com. If you don't want to practice the guided meditation or don't have access to the website, you can instead follow these steps:

1. Take some time to reflect on an emotionally challenging situation that you've experienced in the past.

2. Notice what emotions and bodily sensations are showing up as you reflect.

3. Now, take some time to reflect on an emotionally challenging situation that you're anticipating in the near future.

4. Notice what emotions and bodily sensations are showing up.

5. When you encounter this challenging experience in the future, take a moment to envision the soft, golden light of emotional resilience enveloping you, giving you the strength and flexibility to face this situation with grace and adaptability.

6. Investigate your emotions and sensations with self-compassion and curiosity instead of resisting or suppressing them.

7. Lastly, acknowledge that these feelings are a natural part of your journey toward emotional resilience.

Remember:

- Emotional resilience is your capacity to hold your sail steady as you go through the emotional storms of life.

- It can be strengthened like a muscle through facing challenges head-on and staying calm through them.

- No matter how challenging and uncomfortable a situation may be, you can get through it.

13 Recognizing, Processing, and Regulating Emotions

A GUIDED MEDITATION IN THE RAIN METHOD

THE ABILITY TO RECOGNIZE, ASSESS, monitor, and regulate your emotions will be crucial in becoming independent and emotionally mature. One simple method that you can use to build this skill is RAIN (recognize, allow, investigate, and nurture).

Here's HOW The first step is to simply **recognize (R)** what is going on inside you—perhaps anxious thoughts, guilty feelings, sadness, frustration, tiredness, etc. The second step is to **allow (A)** what is happening by breathing and letting it be. Even though you may not like what you are feeling, your intention is *not* to fix or change anything (and also not to judge yourself for feeling anxious, guilty, etc.). Allowing makes it possible to focus your attention before **investigating (I)** what feels most difficult. The fourth step is to **nurture (N)** yourself by sending a gentle message inward. Finally, you will sit still, letting yourself rest and relax after the RAIN.

Put It Into PRACTICE You can practice RAIN through the guided meditation at EmotionallyImmatureParents.com or by going through these steps:

1. **Recognize:** What are you feeling right now?

2. **Allow:** How can you be with these feelings without trying to fix them or change them? What happens when you just sit with them and let them be?

3. **Investigate:** Where do you feel these feelings in your body (e.g., tightness in your chest or a clenched jaw)? Where is this feeling coming from? Have you felt this way before? What do you need right now (perhaps care and reassurance or a nap)?

4. **Nurture:** Write yourself a gentle, reaffirming, and kind message. Say what you always wanted to hear; let yourself know that you will get through this.

5. **After the RAIN:** Notice any changes or shifts that occurred in the mind, body, and emotions. Write about them.

6. Take a moment to thank yourself for taking the time to practice emotional regulation.

Try practicing RAIN often even when you're not going through a difficult time. With time, the RAIN process will happen faster and more naturally as you encounter uncomfortable emotions and challenging situations. You'll be better able to process and regulate your emotions so you're less emotionally reactive and more in control.

Remember:

- RAIN stands for recognize, allow, investigate, and nurture.
- You can use the RAIN method to process and regulate your emotions.
- Be gentle and kind toward yourself as you're focusing on getting familiar with your feelings and learning how to process and regulate them through RAIN.

14 Continuing to Navigate Uncomfortable Emotions

YOU ARE NOT YOUR FEELINGS

DEPENDING ON YOUR PARENT'S EMOTIONAL maturity level and their relationship with certain feelings, you may have learned to fear, hate, and feel ashamed of experiencing certain feelings at higher degrees than others. Now when you are experiencing an emotion with a particularly negative history, you may instinctively react with guilt, an attempt to flee, or even more of that emotion. This makes it difficult to discern accurate information from your emotion, as it is influenced by the past. To get these old, repeating emotions unstuck and truly process them, you may need to work with more effort and tenderness than with other emotions that don't feel as heavy or triggering.

Here's HOW If you are finding the RAIN activity particularly difficult or have hit a snag as you continue practicing this method, it's time to send some loving-kindness your way. This nurturing approach will help you move through the discomfort.

Put It Into PRACTICE Here's how you can go through RAIN when you're experiencing an extra-challenging emotional storm:

1. Start with step N—nurture. What's a kind and encouraging message that you can tell yourself? What's something loving and reassuring that you need to hear? Write it out.

_____

_____

_____

_____

_____

_____

_____

_____

_____

_____

2. Place a hand or both hands over your chest—your heart center—and say these kind, soothing words out loud or in your mind. Feel the pressure of your hand(s) and the beating of your heart as you say the words.

3. Spend as much time as you need repeating the kind, loving words to yourself as you're feeling into your heart space.

4. Now use the previous activity to go through steps R, A, and I, and spend a few moments just being after the RAIN.

You can be carrying emotional baggage with old emotional reactions linked to events from the past. Something that's currently happening may have triggered the old emotion, giving you inaccurate information about the present-day situation. Use kind words to get back on track to processing and healing from these old, repeating experiences.

Remember:

- Some emotions aren't telling you accurate information.

- These emotions are instead tied to past experiences, and you continue to react to them as though you are going through that experience again.

- When you're feeling stuck, overwhelmed, or resistant while trying to navigate through uncomfortable emotions using RAIN, start with nurture.

15 Expressing Difficult Feelings

PUTTING WORDS TO YOUR EMOTIONS

YOU'RE ONLY RESPONSIBLE FOR HOW you choose to express *your* feelings. Your parent (and everyone else) is responsible for how they choose to express *their* feelings. That said, it's not okay to express feelings in a way that's aggressive, hurtful, manipulative, and/or passive-aggressive. If any of these sound familiar when thinking about how your own parent expressed their feelings when you were growing up, you may have to unlearn those modeled behaviors and learn how to express your feelings in a new, respectful, and productive way. Now that you have worked on releasing fear and shame around experiencing certain feelings in earlier activities, you are ready to discover how you can express your feelings honestly, directly, respectfully, and empathetically.

Here's HOW	There are many healthy ways to express your emotions. These include:
Verbal communication	Clearly articulate your feelings using "I" statements to express your emotions without blaming others.
Emotional boundaries	Set healthy emotional boundaries, allowing yourself to express feelings without taking on others' emotions.
Writing	Journal or write letters about what you feel, even if you never share them.
Art	Draw, paint, or use another creative pursuit as an outlet for your feelings.
Music	Compose, perform, or listen to music that resonates with your emotions.

Dance	Use movement and body language to convey emotions.
Affirmations	Use positive affirmations to validate and express your emotions, building self-acceptance and emotional resilience.
Physical activity	Exercise or engage in sports to channel emotions such as stress or anger.
Therapy	Speak with a mental health professional about your emotions and get guidance in sharing those emotions with others.
Support groups	Join a support group to share your emotions with others who may be experiencing similar feelings.

Put It Into PRACTICE   Follow these steps to express your emotions:

1. Identify the emotions that you were scared of seeing your parent go through and those that you are uncomfortable with yourself today. Use the emotional wheel to help you recognize these feelings.

2. Review the previous list of ways to express your feelings and select the ones that resonate with or interest you.

3. Practice expressing your emotions using your chosen method(s) consistently, making a habit of addressing and processing your emotions in a healthy and respectful manner.

Remember:

● Your emotions are neither good nor bad; they provide valuable information about your internal and external environment.

● It's essential to express your feelings in a respectful, honest, and empathetic manner.

● There are multiple ways to express your emotions, so find the methods that work best for you.

● Consistently practicing healthy emotional expression will help build up your emotional resilience and strengthen your relationships.

16 Tending Your Emotional Needs
THE POWER OF EMPATHY

IN PART 1, YOU LEARNED about the importance of empathy and how it's the key ingredient for a deep emotional connection between you and your parent. It's through a parent's empathy that you feel safe, cared for, connected, seen, heard, and understood.

As a child of an emotionally immature parent, you may still be unconsciously seeking, wishing, and silently (or not so silently) demanding for your parent to pay attention to you, try to understand you, and listen to and support you through emotional challenges in your adult life. However, they may not have the empathy to provide for your emotional needs. You might also be overly empathetic toward your parent and other adults in your life while neglecting yourself in an attempt to change them or finally receive empathy back. But before you can find adults who are capable of the empathy you need, you'll have to rein your energy and love back in and direct empathy toward *yourself* as well as get comfortable experiencing and receiving empathy.

Here's HOW Empathy happens through paying attention, seeking to understand, suspending judgment and criticism, supporting, and investing time, energy, and resources. It'll require you to prioritize yourself: spending time with yourself, treating yourself kindly, talking to yourself gently, encouraging yourself like a best friend, and reassuring yourself.

Put It Into PRACTICE Start by noticing what empathy looks and sounds like for you, then consider how to do and say these things for yourself:

1. Is there an intimate relationship in your life where you do feel empathy from the other person? This can include someone from the past, someone who has passed on, or a beloved pet.

2. What is it about this person that makes you feel safe, loved, cared for, and understood? What do they do or say? Give reassuring glances or long hugs? Listen well? Ask questions? Cheer you up when you're down?

3. How can you do the same for yourself? What can you say to yourself? What can you do for yourself?

4. How can you incorporate these things into each week?

Empathy is a skill that starts with yourself. Directing empathy toward yourself helps satisfy your emotional needs of feeling safe, loved, cared for, and understood.

Remember:

- Everyone has emotional needs.

- Your emotionally immature parent may have lacked empathy and was unable to provide you with your emotional needs.

- You can practice empathy and be empathetic toward yourself by prioritizing yourself, paying attention to your inner world, understanding yourself, and treating yourself well.

CHAPTER 6

Waking Up and Meeting Reality

Optimizing Your Mind for Happiness and Peace

Your mindset sets the stage for how you see *and* approach the world around you. It's important to have the mindset that encourages happiness and peace instead of negativity and stress, etc. In this chapter, you will be rewiring your brain to cultivate a mindset of happiness, gratitude, peace, and growth. You'll learn how to let go of your inner critic. You'll also say goodbye to perfectionism, better handle making mistakes, and even begin appreciating those quirks you once hid and felt ashamed of. Lastly, you'll let go of self-limiting beliefs that you might've inherited from your emotionally immature parent. These activities will prepare you for the next step: becoming your authentic self.

17 Rewiring Your Brain

APPRECIATING THE GOOD, BAD, AND EVERYTHING IN BETWEEN

DUE TO EMOTIONAL IMMATURITY, YOUR parent may have a black-and-white mindset about things: Everything is either right or wrong, good or bad. To them, there is no in-between. If this rings true to your experience, you might have adopted this way of thinking yourself in childhood. Perhaps you find it difficult to see the positives in situations and mostly focus on the negatives. Or you see mistakes as terrible and find yourself very harsh with other people making mistakes around you. However, both successes and mistakes are natural steps to personal and relationship growth. So it's time to begin seeing the positive, negative, and everything in between in a new light. Every situation has something to offer.

Here's HOW Journaling can bring awareness to your inner dialogue and challenge old, inaccurate ways of thinking. This is a very powerful way to challenge a negative or black-and-white mindset and overcome the fear of making mistakes.

Put It Into PRACTICE

1. Grab a journal or a blank piece of paper. Either set a timer for 5 minutes or plan to write until you fill up the entire page.

2. Now bring to mind a situation either of a past challenging event or a future situation that stirs up emotional discomfort. Write whatever thoughts that come up. Don't think too hard and just let the words in your head flow out onto the page.

3. After writing, ask yourself these questions:

- What am I the most afraid of in this situation?

- Have I been through a similar situation before? If so, how did that play out?

- If I made a mistake, what can I learn from it?

- How can I approach this situation differently next time with this lesson in mind?

- If I reached out to a friend about this situation, what soothing, supportive, and encouraging words would they tell me?

- What's the best-case scenario for this situation?

- Has a positive result ever happened in similar situations in the past?

- Even if the worst case (what I'm most afraid of) does happen, will I survive? Will I remember this in one month? Six months? One year? Five years?

You may be experiencing less fear and worrying already, though it'll take some time, consistency with challenging your old, negative ways of thinking, and practice for your outlook to really shift.

Remember:

- Your emotionally immature parent might have thought distortions like black-and-white thinking, which is common with emotional immaturity.

- Because of this and other life experiences, you might have inaccurate ways of thinking, like focusing more on the negatives while dismissing or discounting the positives.

- There are always positives and negatives found within every situation.

- Mistakes happen all the time, and they're natural steps in growing and learning.

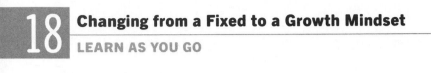

18 Changing from a Fixed to a Growth Mindset

LEARN AS YOU GO

A FIXED MINDSET IS BELIEVING that you can't change, you can't learn new things, you can't improve, and you're stuck with your old habits. The saying "you can't teach an old dog new tricks" is a representation of a fixed mindset. You might've heard your emotionally immature parent use this or other similar sayings to defend and further solidify their own fixed state of mind. However, this idea is just not true. Your brain is neuroplastic: It is always changing. Even as you age, it continues to have lots of capacity for growth. Adopting a growth mindset—believing that you can always learn, ask for help, and practice—will set you up to achieve the changes you want.

Here's HOW Changing your perspective will not happen overnight. It will take consistent reminders, like affirmations, and putting yourself in uncomfortable situations that provide opportunities to learn and see just how wrong that fixed mindset is.

Put It Into PRACTICE

1. Start with affirmations. Here are some examples to get you started. Write them down and put them in places where you will see them regularly. You can alter them however you want or create new ones that resonate more with you.

    ● The only thing that is permanent is change.

- I welcome mistakes, as they're stepping stones on my growth and healing journey.

- I will never know everything, and that's okay. I can always ask for help.

- It's never too late to learn new tricks.

2. This week, choose an uncomfortable situation that involves learning something new (with lots of opportunities for making mistakes). It can be as simple as putting your hand up in class to ask a question. You could ask your boss or supervisor for their feedback. Maybe you could learn a new hobby or skill, like singing, knitting, gardening, etc.

3. Read your affirmations either out loud or to yourself before, during, and after the situation.

Repeat this practice regularly.

Remember:

- A fixed mindset is believing that you can't change, learn new things, make mistakes, or break out of old habits.

- Emotionally immature parents tend to have a fixed mindset, which you might have inherited.

- Your brain continues to change as you age.

- A growth mindset is one where you believe you can change, learn new things, and learn from your mistakes and failures as you continue to grow and heal.

- Positive affirmations and putting yourself in uncomfortable situations are how you can shift to a growth mindset.

19 Giving Up Perfectionism

APPRECIATE FAILURE

PERFECTIONISM CAN BE IMPORTANT TO a parent who is emotionally imma-ture. Perhaps your own parent was/is a perfectionist. Maybe they constantly compared you with your siblings, other family members, etc. or were very critical of things you did or said. Over time, you might've developed the belief that you needed to be perfect to get their approval. This focus on per-fection can continue to impact your relationships, work, and how you feel about yourself now. You may beat yourself up over every mistake (there's that toxic shame again) or ignore the insights of a failure in your desire to get everything just right as soon as possible.

The truth is that no one is perfect. We are all imperfect, flawed human beings who make mistakes and don't know everything. Learning from your mistakes can help you handle these setbacks better and grow as a person.

Here's HOW In this exercise, you are going to break free from perfectionism by reframing your perspective when it comes to failing and making mistakes. You are going to turn your beliefs around to see failing and making mistakes as helpful stepping stones to your success.

Put It Into PRACTICE

1. Think about a recent time that you made a mistake or you failed at something and felt really bad about it—maybe even felt ashamed and humiliated. What happened?

   _____

   _____

2. What thoughts were going through your head at that time?

_____

_____

_____

_____

3. Were you missing any important information? Did you know how to do whatever it was that you were doing? Is there anyone you can ask for help in the future?

_____

_____

_____

_____

4. Looking back, what did you learn from this failure/mistake?

_____

_____

_____

_____

5. Did you make any changes afterward? If not, what can you do differently next time?

_____

_____

_____

_____

6. What's a positive affirmation you can repeat to yourself when it comes to handling mistakes? For example, "I welcome mistakes because they are stepping stones to my growth!"

_____

_____

_____

_____

This will be a process and will take time and effort to change your mindset from perfectionism to appreciating mistakes. Fail lots. Get back up. And fail some more. You will discover another tool to help alleviate perfectionism in Part 3.

Remember:

- Perfectionism means having unreachable standards, constantly comparing yourself to these standards, and feeling bad about yourself when you inevitably make mistakes.

- You are a human being: You are imperfect, you are flawed, and you don't know everything. And this is okay. This is human.

- Mistakes and failures are necessary for learning, growing, and changing. They are stepping stones to success.

20 Cultivating a Happier Mind

THE ATTITUDE OF GRATITUDE

YOUR BRAIN HAS FOUR MAIN attitude highways: negativity, positivity, gratitude, and mindfulness. Just like on a real highway, you can only be driving along one of them at a time. You may have grown accustomed to taking the negative highway—it's easy to get to, and it's the highway that your emotionally immature parent might have shown you. Meanwhile, the other highways can be forgotten. Maybe you even forgot how to get to them. You started taking the mindfulness and positivity highway more in Chapter 4. Making gratitude a more regular route in your brain as well will allow you to experience joy in everyday life and truly appreciate each step in the journey to healing.

Here's HOW Rewiring your brain toward gratitude rather than negativity is about simple, repetitive training. In the following exercise, you will start this training. Keep at it as you continue through this book and afterward. Over time, gratitude will be a more natural path you take without even thinking about it.

Put It Into PRACTICE Starting tomorrow, when you wake up in the morning each day, say to yourself, "Today's going to be a great day" ten times and then "Thank you" ten times. Even if you don't feel like it. Even if it feels fake. Even if you feel tired and terrible. Even if you forget and remember hours later. Say it anyways.

You can also deepen your gratitude practice by keeping a gratitude journal. Here are some examples of what you can write in your gratitude journal every day:

- In the morning: three things that you're grateful for going into the day (experiences, people, material objects, etc.).

- At night: three things that you're grateful for from today.

- A recent bad experience you had that you can also be grateful for.

- Someone who you can say thanks to this week.

- Something about yourself that you can be grateful for (good health, humor, desire to grow and heal, etc.).

The attitude of gratitude is within you. You just need to unlock it.

Remember:

- Gratitude is hardwired in your brain, but it may not be active.

- Gratitude is finding happiness and appreciation for what's already here rather than zeroing in on what's wrong and what's missing.

- You can activate your own attitude of gratitude by saying thank you every morning and keeping a daily gratitude journal.

21 Embracing Your Inner Critic

BEFRIENDING AND ACCEPTING THE ENEMY

REPETITIVE NEGATIVITY CAN BE LIKE having the worst parts of your emotionally immature parent living rent-free in your mind. These thoughts can contain harsh, punishing, shaming, discouraging, criticizing, and mean words that your parent might've said to you. They are also thoughts that you have likely repeated to yourself so many times across so many years that they have become your own inner voice—that inner critic inside your mind. As you learned in Chapter 2, part of your healing will involve facing this critic and breaking free from its negativity.

Here's HOW How can you recognize and free yourself from the negativity? By first getting familiar with the things your inner critic says, then practicing speaking more encouragingly toward yourself. You wouldn't say something so hurtful to your best friend, would you? So why say it to yourself? Encouraging yourself through your challenges and obstacles, whether inside your head or out loud, will create and feed the loving best friend inside of you.

Put It Into PRACTICE

1. Bring to mind a best friend, a beloved sibling, a caring teacher, a dear pet, or anyone who brings you joy (even if you don't know them personally). Who is it?

_____

_____

2. Now think back to a recent situation where you were beating yourself up about something. What were the negative thoughts going through your mind? Perhaps "I suck at this," "You always mess things up," "Why are they treating me this way?"

_____

_____

3. Imagine your chosen person was there. What encouraging words might they tell you? What encouraging words would you want them to tell you?

_____

_____

4. Say the words from the last step out loud.

5. Repeat these encouraging words the next time you encounter a challenging situation that brings up negative thoughts. (To better remember them, you can write them out on Post-it notes and stick them somewhere that you'll see them often, like around a mirror.)

It will take time and consistent effort to change the soundscape of your mind from sounding like a mean, harsh inner critic to a kind, encouraging, and loving best friend. Return to this activity as often as you can, and notice how your inner voice changes.

Remember:

- You can be like your own best friend or you can be like your own worst enemy—it is about how you talk to yourself.

- Being aware of the negative inner critic is the first step to diminishing its power over you.

- Encouraging yourself and talking to yourself like your best friend would talk to you is how you can change your inner voice.

22 Letting Go of Self-Limiting Beliefs, Part 1
THE KEYWORDS OF DOUBT

You picked up beliefs starting at a very young age from your parents and other family members, and then from school, friends, and society. The tricky thing about beliefs is that they're not all true. You might've picked up some false beliefs from your emotionally immature parent; for example: "I am not good enough," "I am unlovable or unworthy of love and affection," "I must be perfect to be accepted or valued," or "I have no control over my life or circumstances."

These false beliefs can be really self-limiting. They keep you from noticing the doors of possibility and opportunity right in front of you—even when the doors are wide open. To let go of these self-limiting beliefs, you first have to become aware of them. Once you become aware of your self-limiting beliefs, you can work to transform them into new, self-empowering beliefs.

Here's HOW There are certain keywords that can reveal what self-limiting beliefs you might have. You will use these keywords as a starting point to reflect on how you've been limiting yourself and where uncomfortable emotions show up and impede your life.

Put It Into PRACTICE The keywords to look out for in self-limiting beliefs are:

- "Should" and "shouldn't"
- "Must" and "mustn't"
- "Can't"
- "Have to"
- "Always"

1. Where in your life do these keywords come up for you? (For example: "I shouldn't change my job." "I must always put others' needs before my own." "I have to please everyone to be liked and accepted." "I'll always mess things up.")

_____

_____

_____

_____

_____

2. What self-limiting belief do you have that's at the root of these thoughts? (For example: "I'll never find a job where I'm paid well _and_ happy." "Others' needs matter more than my own." "I am not worthy of love and acceptance unless I please everyone." "I can never do anything right.")

_____

_____

_____

_____

_____

You will use these reflections to complete the next activity.

Remember:

- Self-limiting beliefs are often passed down to you.
- They can be found in the keywords "should," "shouldn't," "must," "mustn't," "can't," "have to," and "always."

23 Letting Go of Self-Limiting Beliefs, Part 2

TURNING "CAN'T" INTO "CAN"

NOW THAT YOU HAVE IDENTIFIED your self-limiting beliefs in the previous activity, it's time to work on transforming them into new, self-empowering beliefs. By changing your beliefs, you open doors to new possibilities and opportunities in your life.

Here's HOW You can reframe self-limiting beliefs by flipping their negative assumptions, creating new, empowering beliefs that align with your true desires. You can then reinforce these beliefs through daily positive affirmations, internalizing them as a natural part of your thought process. As you take in these new beliefs, notice encouraging shifts in your mindset and behavior patterns. These can lead to a more positive mindset, increased confidence, inner growth, and new opportunities previously blocked by self-limiting beliefs.

Put It Into PRACTICE

1. List the self-limiting beliefs you identified in the previous activity. Alternatively, you can focus on one belief you identified that you feel holds you back more than the others.

_____

_____

2. Now flip those beliefs around. For example: "There is a job out there for me where I'm paid well and happy." "I can prioritize my own needs while still being considerate of others." "I can be my authentic self, and those who truly care about me will appreciate and accept me." "Mistakes are opportunities to learn and grow; I am capable of success and improvement."

3. Repeat these new beliefs out loud to yourself as many times as you need (especially when you feel doubtful) to shift your energy toward more confidence.

4. Lastly, here are two powerful encouraging and opportunity-revealing questions to ask yourself every day, especially when you feel tempted to give up on something because you think it is unattainable or impossible for you. (Be patient, as the answer may not show up right away.)

    ● "Can't I…" (e.g., "Can I be worthy without pleasing everyone?")

    ● "How can I…" (e.g., "How can I land a job that pays well and I'm happy in?")

5. As you regularly change your "can't"s to "can"s, notice how your overall mindset shifts over time.

Remember:

● Challenging and transforming self-limiting beliefs can open doors to new possibilities and opportunities.

● Beliefs can be changed by reinforcing new, empowering beliefs through positive affirmations.

● As you adopt these new beliefs, notice any shifts in your mindset and behavior patterns.

24 Cultivating Happiness and Peace

INTENTIONAL PAUSES

Your PARENT MIGHT NOT HAVE modeled to you the importance of slowing down and taking pauses throughout the day. This can be common of emotionally immature parents as they tend to struggle with self-regulation, emotional awareness, and stress management. Instead, they might've neglected themselves, worked themselves to exhaustion, or chased happiness through career achievements, praise from other family members, being productive, and keeping busy all the time. Perhaps they expected the same from you. However, the happiness that they taught you to chase in other people or jobs, and the peace that they neglected for themselves, doesn't require external circumstances: Both joy and peace can be found within—at any time.

Here's HOW Taking intentional breaks throughout the day to bring yourself back to the present and tune into happiness will help sustain you in the short *and* long term. Some of the benefits include better stress management, improved focus and productivity, and improved mental and emotional well-being. You may be naturally wired to focus on the negatives or keep yourself busy or look for happiness outside of yourself, but with mindful practice, you can shift your mindset and welcome joy and contentment whenever you want it.

Put It Into PRACTICE You can do this practice anywhere that you feel comfortable while sitting. In a quiet place in your home, while you're taking a break at work, and even in public like on a bus. Follow these steps once seated:

1. Close your eyes if you feel comfortable doing so. Place one hand on your heart center and the other hand on your belly.

2. Notice your natural moving breath for a moment.

3. Take a deep inhale and sigh it out with sound.

4. Repeat these deep inhales and sighs a few more times.

5. Imagine a happy memory or bring to mind someone who cares about you and makes you smile just thinking about them (this could be a person or even a beloved pet).

6. Vividly picture the memory or your chosen person or pet for at least 30 seconds upward to 10 minutes.

7. Let go of the image.

8. Notice your natural breath again for a few moments before blinking open your eyes.

You can practice this daily, especially whenever you're feeling exhausted, overworked, and/or fixated on the future.

Remember:

- Happiness and peace can be found within.
- Taking intentional breaks throughout your day is key for short- and long-term sustainability.
- You can train your mind to invite joy and peace simply through focused attention and vivid imagination.

CHAPTER 7

A Life of Freedom

Becoming Emotionally Mature, Authentic, and Free

Emotional maturity, authenticity, and freedom are essential for foster-ing self-awareness, genuine connections with yourself and others, and personal growth. By focusing on these themes, you can break free from unhealthy patterns, cultivate resilience and emotional well-being, and build fulfilling relationships, ultimately transforming yourself and your life. In this chapter, you'll be discovering just what it means to become emotionally mature, authentic, and free—and how to get there. You'll learn about new rules to create greater freedom in your life. You'll gain a greater understanding of emotional boundaries and what you're respon-sible and not responsible for. You'll practice taking things less personally in order to be more in control of your responses and find out how to com-municate vulnerably and genuinely. Lastly, you'll connect with your true, authentic self—and explore your future self.

25 Becoming Emotionally Mature
FIFTEEN RIGHTS TO LIVE BY

GROWING UP WITH AN EMOTIONALLY immature parent, you may not have been taught about the rights that you have as an individual. This is likely because your parent didn't respect or practice these guidelines themselves. If anything, they might've trespassed, denied, ignored, and dismissed these rights that you should've had as you were growing up and reaching adulthood. These rights can act as a first step to claiming your independence and becoming emotionally mature now.

Here's HOW The following are the fifteen rights to live by. You will use this list as you complete the activity in the next section. Keep in mind that this is not an exhaustive list of *every* right to live by in life; it is a starting place for you as you're reclaiming your independence and becoming emotionally mature.

YOU HAVE THE RIGHT TO:

1. Think what you think.

2. Feel what you feel.

3. See and hear what you see and hear.

4. Be yourself and express yourself.

5. Make choices that are healthiest for you.

6. Set boundaries and choose how much to give.

7. Be kind to yourself.

8. Stand up for yourself.

9. Make mistakes and learn.

10. Be respected.

11. Change your mind and navigate old relationships in new ways.

12. Walk away from unhealthy relationships.

13. Bring up issues that need to be solved.

14. Support others in your own capacity.

15. Not want or need anything from your parent.

Put It Into PRACTICE Reflect on the fifteen rights here, and use your insights to start living by the rights that you deserve.

1. As you were reading the list of rights, which of them brought you a sense of freedom?

_____

_____

_____

_____

_____

2. Which of these rights feel hard for you to believe in?

_____

_____

_____

_____

_____

3. What do you do or say—or not do or say—that goes against your own rights?

_____

_____

_____

4. Based on your answer to the previous question, what is it that you need to start doing or saying to be in alignment with your rights?

_____

_____

_____

5. What do you do or say that's in alignment to your rights and that you can continue in the future?

_____

_____

_____

Remember:

- You might've been taught by your parent that you don't have some of these rights. Some of these rights might've been violated, disrespected, ignored, and denied back then—and still today.

- Keeping these rights in mind will help you figure out what goes against your independence.

- To become emotionally mature and independent you will have to believe in these rights, act accordingly, and stand up for them when they are not being respected.

26 Seeking Out Positive Experiences

EMOTIONALLY MATURE RELATIONSHIPS

RELATIONSHIPS DO TAKE SOME WORK, but they shouldn't constantly feel draining, frustrating, disrespectful, and one-sided. Based on your experiences with emotional immaturity, it might be difficult for you to recognize what's healthy versus unhealthy in your relationships. Unhealthy behaviors like being controlling, taking advantage of others, and being codependent might have been taught as the norm in your childhood.

Your journey to becoming emotionally mature and independent will require a shift toward healthier relationships with yourself, your parent, other emotionally immature adults in your life, and possibly new relationships with emotionally mature adults. A simple step in this direction, having positive experiences can remind you of the importance and possibilities of growth, happiness, support, and enjoyment with other people.

Here's HOW The following are examples of positive experiences. Take a look, and use these examples as you reflect in the next section:

- Saying no, setting boundaries, and having them received with acceptance and understanding.

- Sharing differences in opinions without attacking each other's character.

- Experiences of empathy and intimacy: Feeling respected, understood, seen, heard, accepted, safe, cared for, etc.

- Compromising well and fairly.

- Feeling excited to spend time with them again.

- A sense of accountability for making mistakes (e.g., genuine apologies, making amends, and doing better next time).

- Feeling like you can just be yourself around them. They might not always understand you, but that's okay; they accept you just as you are, and you accept them too.

- A sense of trust, honesty, and vulnerability. Even if you are scared of sharing how you're truly thinking or feeling, you do it anyways.

Put It Into
PRACTICE

1. Identify which of the previous examples you have experienced recently and in what relationships.

2. In what relationships have you not been having these experiences? What has been happening instead?

3. What can you do within your current relationships to have more positive experiences?

You can't change other people, force them to change, or make them understand, but you can change how *you* behave.

Remember:

● Relationships do take some work, but they shouldn't feel draining, frustrating, and one-sided most of the time.

● Your journey in becoming emotionally mature and independent will require you to work with your relationships to make them healthier.

● Positive experiences at a deeper emotional level are a helpful guide as you look at what needs changing in your relationships.

● You can't change people or force them to change, but you can change your own behaviors and possibly inspire change in those around you.

27 Taking Things Less Personally, Part 1

IT'S NOT ALWAYS ABOUT YOU

WHEN IT COMES TO DEALING with an emotionally immature parent or other emotionally immature adults in your life, they will do or say things from time to time that you take offense to. You may actually be more sensitive to their words than you are to other people's. It feels easy for you to take their behavior personally. You can learn to stop taking things personally and become less reactive in the process.

Here's HOW Affirmations and reminders are a helpful tool when you're taking something personally and feeling triggered and reactive. They can help you reframe your thoughts from negative thought patterns and beliefs to more positive and constructive ones, help you with emotional regulation, and reinforce self-awareness so you can identify that you're being triggered, giving you more time to respond rather than react.

Put It Into PRACTICE

1. Repeat this affirmation to yourself for a short period of time (follow your instinct in how long you repeat it, listening to how your mindset shifts as you do) the next time you feel resentful, defensive, and hurt by your parent or another person and might be taking something personally: "Don't take this personally. It isn't always about me. Their behavior is more about them than about me. What they said or did has more to say about their emotional history than about me in that moment."

2. Write out this affirmation on a piece of paper and stick it somewhere like on a mirror or put it as a note on your phone that you'll see often.

Write down your observations.

_____

_____

_____

_____

_____

_____

_____

_____

_____

_____

_____

_____

_____

_____

Remember:

- It's not always about you.

- Your parent's (and other people's) behaviors and reactions sometimes say more about them than about you.

- People often act out of their own emotional histories, attitudes, and perspectives.

28 Taking Things Less Personally, Part 2

WHAT TO DO WHEN IT IS ABOUT YOU

IF USING THE AFFIRMATIONS AND reminders in the previous activity don't resolve the negative emotions you have, try self-reflection. Maybe in this instance it *is* about you, and there are possible actions and solutions that you use with the person to mend the issue and move forward together.

Here's HOW Self-reflection can help you identify if there is any truth to what your parent or another person is saying, and if there is, how you can take responsibility for your actions and work toward resolving the issue.

Put It Into PRACTICE Reflect on the following:

1. Is there some truth to what they said about me? Is there something here that I need to take responsibility for? Is there something here that I can work on?

2. Is there something that I need, want, or have been expecting from them that I haven't clearly told them about?

3. What might have led them to act or say what they did? What might they have felt in that moment?

_____

_____

_____

4. If this isn't a recurring issue, can I give them grace and understanding? How?

_____

_____

_____

5. Or do I need to let them know how their action made me feel? Is there a boundary here that I need to set?

_____

_____

_____

Using what insights you uncovered while reflecting, practice being vulnerable by communicating openly and honestly with the other person. Express how their behavior or words made you feel and listen to their perspective. Work together to find a resolution that works for both parties.

Remember:

- Reflect on the situation before taking any action.

- Try to see the situation from the other person's perspective.

- Take responsibility for your actions or words if necessary.

- Communicate openly and honestly with the person involved to find a resolution.

29 Letting Go of Self-Limiting Identities
MEETING YOUR TRUE, AUTHENTIC SELF

As you learned from Chapter 2, your parent might be shame-based, acting out of their deep inner spiritual wound of "I am bad." It's likely you were made to play rigid, false roles to help keep the shame-based family system running. It is draining and soul-sucking to continue wearing these masks and pretending to be these characters. And it hides who you really are! In order for you to shed these masks, you'll have to first recognize what roles you were playing—and may still be playing today.

Here's HOW Self-awareness and self-reflection will help you identify these old masks that you no longer want to put on. This kind of self-inquiry, as well as engaging in interactions and having new experiences, will be your ongoing journey in discovering who you truly are.

Put It Into PRACTICE Revisit Chapter 1 and read through the list of false roles. Take note of the roles that stand out for you and that you feel you had to play. (There may be roles that aren't on the list that you had to play. Make up your own names for these.)

1. Write the roles:

   _____

   _____

2. Are you still playing any of these roles today? Which ones?

   _____

   _____

3. How would a near and dear friend describe you?

4. How would you want to be remembered? What would you want to be written on your epitaph?

5. What words and images come to mind when you think about yourself?

6. Using the answers to the previous questions, create new and more accurate identities for yourself (e.g., nature lover, coffee enthusiast, big and bubbly ball of energy).

Remember:

- In a shame-based family system, everyone is given rigid roles to play.

- These false roles that you were made to play (and you might still be playing today) are not who you truly are.

- Discovering your true, authentic self will require you to separate these masks from the person beneath them.

30 Honing the Art of Self-Expression

THE FACE FRAMEWORK

YOU WILL INEVITABLY DISAPPOINT OTHERS when you're being true to yourself. Your true thoughts and feelings will not always match your parent's expectations of you. Your parent may not understand (or want to understand) why you think or feel the way that you do, and that's okay. Part of being authentic is respecting and accepting each other in your uniqueness and differences. You are only responsible for yourself and whether or not you choose to be honest about who you truly are. It's time to shine as your real self.

Here's HOW You can nurture your unique, authentic self through continually facing your fears and discomforts with how others might react to you. You also become more confident through this process. The FACE (firm, authentic, compassionate expression) framework is a powerful method for pushing through these fears and discomforts to show the world who you are. It has three parts:

1. Practice communicating with **firmness** by clearly and assertively conveying your thoughts, feelings, and needs without being aggressive, passive, or allowing others to dominate the conversation.

2. Practice being **authentic** and true to yourself by embracing your unique qualities, personality, strengths, and weaknesses while maintaining honesty, transparency, and integrity in your relationships and daily interactions.

3. Practice **compassionate expression** by communicating your thoughts, feelings, and needs in a way that is sensitive, empathetic, and understanding toward both yourself and others.

Put It Into PRACTICE The next time you have something you want to express, whether to your parent or someone else, follow these steps:

1. **Do a self-reflection:** Know clearly what your goal is before interacting with your parent, and keep it simple. This is especially important when it comes to letting your emotionally immature parent know how you are feeling or what you are thinking. It may be unrealistic to aim for a genuine connection, positive feedback, or for them to be vulnerable in return because they are lacking emotional intelligence, sensitivity, communication skills, and empathy. For example, maybe you need to tell your parent that you won't be coming home this Christmas. Your goal here could be just to feel good for expressing yourself and let go of responsibility for your parent's reaction.

2. **Set the stage:** Choose a calm environment and minimize distractions before communicating.

3. **Apply the FACE framework:** Maintain firmness by communicating clearly and assertively, express thoughts and feelings authentically, and show compassion, empathy, and understanding. (Some tips to help you communicate with more compassion include using "I" statements, being present, practicing nonjudgment, validating their emotions, choosing your words carefully, encouraging open dialogue, and practicing patience.)

Remember:

- Your true thoughts and feelings are valid, even though others may not always receive them with respect, understanding, and acceptance.

- You're only responsible for your actions, words, and feelings; you're not responsible for other people's actions, words, and feelings.

- You get to choose whether to be honest with yourself and others.

- Try your best, practice, and learn from any mistakes.

31 | Choosing Authenticity over Conformity

IT'S OKAY TO DISAPPOINT OTHERS

WERE YOU ABLE TO *just be yourself* growing up? Did you feel like your parent accepted you for who you were? If the answer to these questions is no, then you might struggle with *just being you* now as an adult. Instead, maybe your experiences as a child have trained you to be a people pleaser, knowing exactly what to say to make others happy, always agreeing, and conforming to their likes and dislikes. Perhaps you never practiced letting others know what you were really thinking or what you like and what you dislike because you didn't want to "disappoint" them. The truth is that you will inevitably disappoint others, including your parent, when you choose to live authentically. While this fear may have held you back in the past, it's time to embrace the truth—and yourself—now.

Here's HOW To break free from this fear of displeasing others, you will need to learn how to handle the disappointment. As you explore this in the following exercise, please give yourself permission to give life—and yourself—a try.

Put It Into PRACTICE

1. Is there any area in your life where you are holding yourself back? Maybe a wild dream, small goal, or hobby/interest that you've always wanted to pursue, but you haven't acted on yet?

_____

_____

_____

2. Are you worried, afraid, or feeling guilty about how someone will react if you do pursue this? Who comes to mind? Your parent? Your partner? Your friend? Strangers?

_____

_____

_____

_____

3. What's the worst-case scenario?

_____

_____

_____

_____

4. What's the best-case scenario?

_____

_____

_____

_____

5. What if you firmly believed that you can't control the outcome, you can't 100 percent predict the outcome, and you are not responsible for their emotional reaction? What would you do differently?

_____

_____

_____

_____

6. How can you take an actionable step toward living your authentic life with this information in mind? For example, maybe you have always dreamed of traveling solo. An actionable step that you can take would be asking advice from someone who's done it.

_____

_____

_____

_____

_____

7. Once you have taken the step in the previous question, reflect on how it felt and what next steps you can take and when.

_____

_____

_____

_____

_____

Remember:

- Behind your self-doubt and fears of disappointing others lives your authentic life, your authentic self.

- You will inevitably disappoint others, including your parent, when you start living a life that's true to yourself.

- Learn to handle disappointing others by letting go of control over the outcome, not assuming you can 100 percent predict the outcome, and not taking responsibility for their emotional reactions.

32 Giving Yourself Permission

SELF-TRUST

YOU EXPLORED LETTING GO OF self-limiting beliefs in the previous chapter by becoming aware of your own limiting words and choosing not to use them. Another factor that might be holding you back from becoming truly independent is a need for external validation. It's natural to look to others for approval. And while it's wise to seek out other people's advice, opinions, ideas, and suggestions, you also need to listen to yourself. Learn to trust yourself and give yourself permission to try something new, explore your desires, take risks, and get what you need—regardless of what other people may think.

Here's HOW Identifying where in your life you have been giving away your power is a great start. When it comes to your relationship with your parent, where have you been seeking validation and approval? What decisions have you been making or not making based on your parent's desires and expectations rather than your own desires? How have you been seeking permission from your parent and/or other people in your life to pursue small or big dreams that you have?

Put It Into PRACTICE In this activity, you will take back the power and give yourself permission to be authentic. You can do this by following the guided meditation provided at EmotionallyImmature Parents.com. If you don't want to practice the guided meditation or don't have access to the website, you can do the visualization on your own with these steps:

1. Imagine that for an entire day you only need your own permission to do *anything*. You aren't worried about disappointing others, being judged by others, or how they might react to your decisions. You don't have to tell anyone else what you're doing and why you're doing it.

2. How would *you* choose to spend your day?

3. Reframe your answer as a positive affirmation that begins, "On this day I would give myself permission to…" For example, "On this day I would give myself permission to sleep in and wake up when I felt like it. I would give myself permission to take myself out for a nice breakfast. I would give myself permission to walk on streets around my neighborhood that I've never explored…" You can do this daily, giving yourself permission and trusting your wants, needs, and desires. You can repeat this affirmation especially when you are doubting yourself or if you find yourself seeking external validation, permission, and approval.

Remember:

- It's natural to seek validation from others, but you also need to trust yourself.

- You can give yourself permission to do and be you.

- Identifying where in your life that you've been giving away your power and seeking other people's validation and approval is a great place to start reclaiming that power.

33 Discovering Your Higher Self
A POWERFUL VERSION OF YOU

GROWING UP WITH AN EMOTIONALLY immature parent, you may not have been allowed to be just as you are. Perhaps you were made to play false roles and were passed down self-limiting beliefs that you weren't even aware of. But your past does not have to define who you are today. Your future is yet unwritten, and it arrives one day at a time. You're powerful beyond measure, and you *can* choose who you become.

Here's HOW Your imagination is one of the most powerful tools that you have in creating a brighter future and realizing your potential. If you can think it, vividly imagine it, feel it, and even *fake it* as if your future dream life and the highest version of yourself are already here—you'll manifest it.

Put It Into PRACTICE Start by vividly imagining that *your higher self* has arrived and you're living your dream life right now. Then write about what your higher self and your dream life look and feel like:

1. Where are you living? What is your home space like? How do you feel in your home?

_____

_____

_____

_____

2. How are you feeling?

_____

_____

_____

_____

3. How are you dressed?

_____

_____

_____

_____

4. How are you talking? What do you sound like? How do others feel talking to you?

_____

_____

_____

_____

5. Has your job changed? If so, what are you doing now? Or if you're still in the same job, how are you feeling differently in your job?

_____

_____

_____

_____

6. What's your daily routine like? How do you spend your free time?

_____

_____

_____

_____

7. Who's around you? Who are you choosing to spend your time with? How do they feel around you?

_____

_____

_____

_____

8. What old habits are you no longer doing?

_____

_____

_____

_____

9. What new habits do you have now?

_____

_____

_____

_____

10. How do you approach challenges, obstacles, and uncomfortable situations differently than before?

_____

_____

_____

_____

_____

_____

_____

_____

_____

_____

_____

_____

Return to this image often and start acting as this future version of you.

Remember:

- Your past doesn't have to define your present and your future.

- Your imagination is one of the most powerful tools that you have in unlocking your potential.

- Spending time and energy feeling into your future self and future dream life and pretending to be like your future self today will help you manifest those desires.

34 Creating New Rights to Live By

A LIFE OF FREEDOM

IF YOU WANT TO BE truly independent, authentic, and free, then you must stick up for and act on the fifteen rights that you learned in Activity 25: Becoming Emotionally Mature. However, the list doesn't stop there. You are the writer of your own story. As this powerful main character and director, you should also create new rights for yourself. These will allow you to cultivate more independence, freedom, and authenticity in your life as you continue to shed what no longer serves you.

Here's HOW To prepare for making new rights, first revisit the fifteen rights in Activity 25: Becoming Emotionally Mature. Let them really sink in. You will use them as you reflect in the next section.

Put It Into PRACTICE

1. How can you make the fifteen rights better suit you? Write out any edits or changes you would make. For example, instead of "the right to stand up for myself" maybe "the right to not tolerate being yelled at."

_____

_____

_____

_____

_____

2. What new rights do you want to add to the list? For example, the right to smile for no reason, the right to cry in public, the right to say no without explanation, or the right to choose the happiest option.

3. How can you start standing up for these rights now?

You are powerful beyond measure. Nobody can take these rights away from you. Reclaim your power if you've been giving it away.

Remember:

● You are the main character and the director of your life.

● The rights that you create for yourself remind and guide you in building a sense of independence, respect, and freedom in your life.

● Nobody can take your rights away, not even your parent.

PART 3

ACTIVITIES FOR MOVING FORWARD WITH EMOTIONAL MATURITY AND BOUNDARIES

Now that you have worked to accept the realities of life with an emotionally immature parent, you can move along toward your best future. In Part 3, you'll continue healing through becoming more loving and accepting toward yourself and your parent, discover inner child work and how to let go of shame, and forgive at your discretion. You'll create more self-trust and trust within your relationships, learn how to set and maintain healthy and firm boundaries, and discover what boundaries are a good fit for you and your needs. Then you'll discover how to keep moving forward in your relationships as you become more independent, handle reactions to your boundaries, rebuild trust when it's broken, hold each other accountable, and create more harmony. Later in this part, you will determine whether you want to reconcile with your parent or establish a more limited relationship, and you will take steps to do so.

As in Part 2, you will want to go through the following activities in order at first. However, feel free to revisit the activities that call back to you along your healing journey. There are also guided meditations scattered throughout the chapters. Give them a try and practice them regularly if you like, to help you cultivate confidence, wisdom, and power within. As you move through these chapters, remember to give yourself and others grace, be gentle, make many mistakes, apologize when necessary, and continue to heal and grow.

CHAPTER 8

Healing the Past

Loving-Kindness, Inner Child Healing, Toxic Shame Release, and Forgiveness

Being loving toward yourself isn't something that feels natural to many people, especially those who have grown up with an emotionally immature parent who didn't teach this self-kindness in their own behavior or words. Instead, you may feel more comfortable with shame and self-criticism. And it may feel easier to focus on negative thoughts and feelings toward those who have hurt you as well. In the long term, this route will not heal your wounds, however. In this chapter, you will invite healing by practicing being more loving and gentler toward yourself and others, connect with and reparent your wounded inner child, release toxic shame, and forgive yourself (and others, if you choose). If you have unprocessed trauma, it's important to make sure you speak with your family doctor or a therapist before embarking on this work. If at any point going through these activities you feel dissociative (like you're detached from your thoughts, emotions, bodily sensations, and/or surroundings), stop the exercise and speak with a healthcare professional.

35 Rediscovering the Love Within

A GUIDED MEDITATION FOR COMPASSION

YOU MIGHT NOT HAVE RECEIVED consistent unconditional love from your parent growing up and it left a void. You may still be unconsciously or consciously seeking that love from them today or from other emotionally immature and unavailable adults. Fortunately, the love that you've been seeking and needing can be grown from within. You can practice *metta* or loving-kindness to be more loving and kinder toward yourself and more loving and kinder toward others, including your parent. Love and kindness are never diminished by being shared—they only keep growing and growing.

Here's HOW Practice loving-kindness through positive affirmations, either as part of meditation or on their own. These four affirmations will allow you to unlock loving-kindness in the following exercise: "May I/you be loved, may I/you be safe, may I/you be happy, and may I/you be free."

Put It Into PRACTICE Practice loving-kindness by following the guided meditation provided at EmotionallyImmatureParents.com. Then answer the reflection questions. If you don't want to practice the guided meditation or don't have access to the website, you can instead repeat these loving-kindness affirmations:

- May I be loved.
- May I be safe.
- May I be happy.
- May I be free.

- May you be loved.
- May you be safe.
- May you be happy.
- May you be free.

Start with directing loving-kindness toward yourself, repeating the "May I…" affirmations out loud or in your mind (infusing each word with love and kindness from your heart). Then bring to mind a loved one (it can be a family member or a friend) and repeat the "May you…" affirmations out loud or in your mind. Next, bring to mind an acquaintance and repeat the "May you…" affirmations out loud or in your mind. Finally, envision the whole planet as you repeat the "May you…" affirmations out loud or in your mind.

After repeating these affirmations for about 6 minutes total, answer the following questions:

1. Was it easy or hard directing loving-kindness toward yourself? What about toward your loved one? Toward an acquaintance or toward the planet?

2. Are there any changes that you would like to make to the four phrases? Maybe they don't fit well with you and you change all of them. Or you make a few alterations so they sound right for you.

3. What emotions came up when you were practicing loving-kindness?

_____

_____

_____

_____

_____

4. Do you notice any shifts within your mind, body, and/or emotions following the practice? If so, what are they?

_____

_____

_____

_____

_____

Take a moment to acknowledge the love and compassion that you have nurtured today. You are lovable just as you are. Choose to be kind by practicing loving-kindness regularly.

Remember:

- You can find the love and kindness you want and need within.

- The more that you love and be kind to yourself, the more you are able to receive love and kindness from others.

- You can practice loving-kindness through these four simple phrases: may I be loved, may I be safe, may I be happy, and may I be free.

- Love and kindness never diminish by being shared—they only keep growing and growing.

36 | Healing Your Inner Child, Part 1
THE WOUNDED, WONDERFUL CHILD WITHIN

YOU WERE ONCE A YOUNG, innocent child who was brought into the world. You went through important developmental stages from infant, to toddler, to preschooler, to grade-schooler, to adolescent. Your parent was given a very difficult role: They were responsible for making sure all your needs were met, loving you, accepting you, paying attention to you, and teaching you important life skills. However, while they might've tried their best, an emotionally immature parent was unable to provide the love and care you needed to bloom.

If your needs weren't met, you were punished, you were shamed, and you didn't feel accepted, seen, or encouraged during your developmental years—particularly the infant, toddler, and/or preschooler stages—you likely have challenges with things like mistrust, shame and doubt, guilt, and inferiority today.

Here's HOW You can have numerous wounded children—younger versions of you—living inside you. The first step to healing these children is recognizing who they are.

Put It Into PRACTICE Answer yes or no to each question. Don't think too hard about your answer; instead, pause and *feel* if it's a yes or a no. The more that you answer yes, the more likely there's a wounded child inside you.

WOUNDED INFANT

1. Do you struggle with getting your own needs met?
   ❏ Yes   ❏ No

2. Do you believe you need someone else to get your needs met for you?
   ❏ Yes   ❏ No

3. Do you have issues trusting yourself and others?
   ❏ Yes   ❏ No

4. Is it hard for you to recognize when you're tired and hungry?
   ❏ Yes   ❏ No

5. Do you often feel like you don't belong?
   ❏ Yes   ❏ No

6. Are you terrified of being abandoned?
   ❏ Yes   ❏ No

WOUNDED TODDLER

1. Do you struggle with knowing what you want and need?
   ❏ Yes   ❏ No

2. Are you afraid to explore new places by yourself?
   ❏ Yes   ❏ No

3. When you're feeling stressed, do you need someone to tell you what to do?
   ❏ Yes   ❏ No

4. Do you fear other people getting angry with you and always try to avoid conflict?
   ❏ Yes   ❏ No

5. Are you excessively critical of others and fear others judging you?
   ❏ Yes   ❏ No

WOUNDED PRESCHOOLER

1. Do you struggle with knowing what you're feeling in the moment?
   ❑ **Yes**   ❑ **No**

2. Do you usually try to control your feelings and other people's feelings?
   ❑ **Yes**   ❑ **No**

3. Do you struggle with expressing your true feelings?
   ❑ **Yes**   ❑ **No**

4. Do you feel responsible for other people's behaviors, decisions, and feelings?
   ❑ **Yes**   ❑ **No**

5. Do you believe that you have the power to change someone else?
   ❑ **Yes**   ❑ **No**

6. Do you believe it's your responsibility to meet your parent's expectations so that they can feel good about themselves?
   ❑ **Yes**   ❑ **No**

Remember:

- You went through important developmental stages when you were younger, during which you had specific needs that only your parent could've helped you meet.

- If you didn't get your needs met and there was punishment, shame, neglect, and abuse, you likely struggle with arrested development (more on this in Chapter 2).

- Mistrust, shame and doubt, guilt, and inferiority can come from your wounded inner child.

37 Healing Your Inner Child, Part 2

CONNECTING WITH YOUR INNER CHILD

THE WOUNDED INNER CHILD/CHILDREN YOU uncovered in the last activity is still seeking unconditional love, encouraging support, and protective energy. You're the adult now, and you can connect with that inner child/children. You can become your own source of love, support, and protection. It all begins with making contact.

Here's HOW To prepare to connect with your inner child, find old pictures of yourself when you were younger. Baby photos. Toddler photos. Preschool and grade school photos. High school photos (the more awkward the better). Can you see how precious and innocent you were as a baby? How full of life you were on the first day of preschool? You might have few memories of your childhood years. If you feel comfortable, you can ask family members about what you were like when you were younger. With these photos, memories, and insights from family in mind, follow the steps in the next section.

Put It Into PRACTICE Start by writing four letters in a journal or on blank pieces of paper: one to your infant self, one to your toddler self, one to your preschool/early grade school self, and one to your adolescent self (thirteen to seventeen years old). Imagine that you're writing these letters as a wise, loving, caring, and protective guardian. In each letter, tell that self how much you love them, appreciate them, and want them, and how you will take care of them. Let them know that you understand the pain, the fear, the confusion, and the difficulties that they had to go through. Say anything that you wanted and needed to hear during those difficult times. (Your letters can be as short as a paragraph or as long as several pages.)

Once you've written the letters, find a quiet and safe place, and read them out loud to yourself. Allow whatever feelings come up to be here. (It's normal to feel sad and perhaps cry during this step because these are words that you've always wanted and needed to hear.)

Write down your observations.

_____

_____

_____

_____

_____

_____

_____

_____

_____

_____

_____

_____

Remember:

- Your wounded inner child needs a guardian—and that guardian is you.

- Set the stage for being your own guardian by looking at old photos of yourself when you were a baby, toddler, preschooler, and grade-schooler.

- If you feel safe, you can ask family members about what you were like when you were younger and listen to stories about yourself.

- Writing loving letters to your wounded inner children is how you can contact them.

38 Healing Your Inner Child, Part 3

GETTING YOUR NEEDS MET THROUGH SELF-CARE

IF YOUR PARENT WAS/IS EMOTIONALLY immature, they might've used you to get their needs met. This was not okay: It was your parent's responsibility to take care of you when you were growing up, not the other way around. Now that you are the adult, you can provide your wounded inner child/children with what they needed.

Here's HOW You can help your wounded inner children meet their needs through different acts of self-care. These intentional, loving acts help your inner child finally meet the needs that weren't met back then. Do these acts often, and follow what feels nurturing for you.

Put It Into PRACTICE Check out the acts of self-care listed here and start trying them out for yourself.

SELF-CARE ACTIVITIES FOR YOUR INFANT:

- Take a hot bath.

- Let yourself eat, snack, and sleep when you're feeling hungry or tired rather than following strict times.

- Gently touch yourself and notice the sensations.

- Let someone hug you or hold you.

SELF-CARE ACTIVITIES FOR YOUR TODDLER:

- Visit a park and let your eyes wander; touch what calls to you.

- Wander around your neighborhood.

- Have a paint night. Paint with your hands; get messy.

- Go to a museum. Notice the colors and details of the paintings.

- Make silly noises with your mouth.

- Grab random objects from your house, bang them together, and make lots of noise.

SELF-CARE ACTIVITIES FOR YOUR PRESCHOOLER:

- Go online and ask whatever questions come to mind.

- Give yourself permission to feel whatever feeling comes up, when it comes up.

- Paint, draw, dance, or sing out your emotions.

- Let yourself daydream and fantasize about your future.

Remember:

- You had specific needs when you were younger that only your parent could've helped you meet.

- You can meet those needs now through self-care activities.

- Allow yourself to be creative in these activities, and give yourself permission to get silly.

39 Healing Your Inner Child, Part 4

REPARENTING YOUR INNER CHILD

YOU WERE LIKE A SPONGE when you were younger: You absorbed everything around you, learning from what you saw and heard, even if your parent didn't intend for that "lesson." You were also egocentric in a way where you made sense of the world around you with your being in the center of it. If your parent was unhappy or stressed, or your parents were constantly fighting, you would've believed it was your fault. Your parent might've even said hurtful words to you that became your own self-limiting thoughts and beliefs. You might not have had the childhood that you deserved with a parent who modeled healthy behaviors and beliefs, but you can reparent yourself—starting today.

Here's HOW Affirmations and visualization are both simple tools that can help you reparent your wounded inner child. With these practices, you can make contact with your inner children and tell them the loving, supportive, and encouraging words that they needed to hear.

Put It Into PRACTICE In this activity, you will use affirmations and visualization by following the guided meditation provided at EmotionallyImmatureParents.com. If you don't want to practice the guided meditation or don't have access to the website, you can instead write out and repeat these positive affirmations or create your own. Read and repeat these words often. You can repeat these affirmations as you're looking at an old photo of your younger self. You can even imagine holding your precious younger self in your arms as you're repeating these affirmations. Have them readily available and remind yourself often of these words, especially when you're going through a difficult time:

- I'm so glad that you were born.

- I love you just as you are.

- I love taking care of you. You don't need to take care of me.

- All your needs are okay with me. I'll take care of all your needs.

- You can feel all your feelings. They're okay with me. I'll never leave you.

- It's okay to think what you think and have different opinions and ideas.

- I'm always here for you no matter what. You can always come to me.

- You can do things your own way.

- You can dress any way that you like.

- You can ask for what you need and what you want.

- You are not responsible for your parent.

- You are not responsible for your parent's emotions; you're not responsible for their happiness, sadness, disappointments, regrets, anger, or pride.

- Your boundaries are okay with me. I'll accept and respect your noes.

Remember:

- You might have learned self-limiting beliefs about yourself from your emotionally immature parent.

- You were an egocentric sponge when you were younger, absorbing your parent's emotions, problems, and reactions and believing it was your fault.

- You can reparent yourself today through telling and reminding yourself loving and encouraging words that you needed to hear back then.

40 Healing Toxic Shame, Part 1

GIVING YOURSELF PERMISSION TO BE IMPERFECT

IN CHAPTER 6, YOU EXPLORED how perfectionism can be stressed to you throughout childhood by an emotionally immature parent. It comes from that deeper toxic shame and can impact how you see failure and making mistakes as an adult. It can also impact how you see yourself. Due to toxic shame, you may have unrealistic standards of yourself and feel embarrassed of your quirks and flaws. As you also learned in Chapter 6, being human means being flawed. It means being unique and imperfect. It's time to let go of that toxic shame and accept yourself just as you are today—quirks and all. The Japanese concept of *wabi-sabi* celebrates the beauty of imperfection, impermanence, and incompleteness. It's the golden cracks of a broken ceramic bowl mended back together with golden glue that makes it beautiful. You are a work of art—a forever unfinished work in progress. Focus on the process rather than the perfect finale.

Here's HOW Someone in the past (like a parent) might've been judgmental and nonaccepting, but that was only their perspective—not the absolute truth. You are acceptable and worthy of love just as you are. Giving yourself permission to be imperfect and recognizing how these imperfections make you unique will help you start to release your toxic shame.

Put It Into PRACTICE

1. What are the characteristics and physical features about yourself that you don't like?

2. Who and/or what in the past told you that these traits are bad?

_____

_____

3. How can you view your imperfections as unique characteristics that contribute to your growth and individuality rather than as a bad trait? For example, impulsivity can be seen as struggling with planning ahead and decision-making or it can be perceived as a gift of spontaneity that nurtures creativity, adaptability, and enthusiasm for new experiences.

_____

_____

4. Say this affirmation out loud: "I give myself permission to be human: imperfect and flawed. I give myself permission to feel however I feel. I give myself permission to make mistakes and fail."

5. Repeat this affirmation ten times.

6. Notice any shifts in emotions and energy in the body after the last step, especially around your chest and upper abdomen.

Revisit this affirmation when you are feeling tempted to judge yourself for being imperfect.

Remember:

- Toxic shame can make you feel as though you have things to be embarrassed of about yourself.

- You are already worthy of love and belonging just as you are.

- Being human means being imperfect.

- Appreciating and accepting your unique flaws and giving yourself permission to be imperfect are how you can start releasing your toxic shame.

41 Healing Toxic Shame, Part 2

BRINGING YOUR DARKNESS TO LIGHT

TOXIC SHAME MAY TELL YOU that there's something bad and even "damaged" inside of you. It may say that if other people truly knew who you are, they'll judge you, reject you, and abandon you. This is because toxic shame grows in secrecy, hiding, and isolation. It wants you to keep it a secret, try to be perfect, hold back from being vulnerable in your relationships, and isolate yourself from genuine connection so it can thrive. The medicine for toxic shame is self-love and self-acceptance: embracing the parts of you that you feel bad about and sharing them with others. It is released through externalizing your shame, having your feelings validated, and being accepted for who you are today.

Here's HOW As you learned earlier, practicing loving-kindness can help you develop self-love and self-acceptance. Here, it will be the medicine for toxic shame.

Put It Into PRACTICE The following are some ways that you can externalize and release your toxic shame. Try out one or more of these activities right now, then schedule the activities that resonated with you into your regular routine:

- Have someone who is accepting and nonjudging in your life hear your story, your struggles, and your mistakes, and validate them.

- Share how you're really feeling with a significant other.

- Join a support group. If you're struggling with addictions, a support group can be especially valuable.

- Journal about painful memories and feel whatever emotions come up. Let yourself cry and grieve if you need to.

- Recognize where you compartmentalize certain roles and areas in your life. Allow those parts to be included in your whole. Embrace, feel into, and talk about them rather than ignoring and denying them.

- Share shameful memories with a nonjudging significant other.

- Write out shaming, judgmental thoughts that you have about yourself.

- Ask for something you want and need.

- Set a boundary and deal with critical and shaming behaviors from the other person.

- Respond to a mistake with acceptance and give yourself permission to be imperfect.

- Make a choice that is true to yourself and handle the disappointment from others.

- Practice a meditation for mindfulness, loving-kindness, shame releasing, or inner child healing.

Remember:
- Toxic shame grows in hiding, secrecy, and isolation.

- Toxic shame is released by externalizing it, validating it, and being accepted for it.

- There are many ways that you can externalize toxic shame. Try these practices regularly.

42 Letting Go of Your Healing Fantasies, Part 1

CHOOSING A PATH THAT'S TRUE TO YOURSELF

As a young child, you might've created a healing fantasy to remain hopeful through the difficulties of having an emotionally immature parent. A childhood healing fantasy involves how one day in the future you're going to do something or fix something or change something in order to be happy and make your parent happy too. Your fantasies can be based on your parent's expectations of you. For example, my childhood healing fantasy was that I would get into medical school and become a doctor so that I would be happy and complete and I would make my parents happy too.

However, even if a fantasy does come true, it doesn't heal you, and it doesn't permanently fix or heal your parent's problems either. The underlying emotional damage from the past still exists. Also, these fantasies are disempowering because they often place the responsibility for healing on external factors, like your parent's behavior, rather than focusing on your inner growth, resilience, and self-healing. You might've been chasing a childhood healing fantasy believing that it'll complete you, fix you, and heal you and your family, but it's not the solution. To truly heal, you can let go of your healing fantasy now and choose a path forward that's more authentic for you.

Here's HOW Recognizing what your childhood healing fantasy is will be the first step in choosing a path forward that's truer to you. While fantasies are often based on your parent's expectations of you (like becoming a doctor), they can also be impacted by society's expectations of you (like having children). They can be related to attaining a specific job, general career success, income, a committed romantic relationship, etc. Use the questions in the next section to uncover the fantasy you have been chasing.

Put It Into
PRACTICE

1. What is your childhood healing fantasy? Here are some common examples: believing if you behave perfectly or meet all your parent's expectations then finally they will provide you with the love, care, and attention that you've been craving; thinking that if you achieve significant success, fame, or recognition then your parent will finally appreciate and validate you; hoping that someone will magically appear in your life and provide you with the emotional support that you need.

2. What have you been pursuing that's based on your parent's expectations of you, your family's expectations of you, or society's expectations of you (or what you think expectations of you are)? There will likely be "should," "have to," or "must" thoughts surrounding this goal, and it's a goal that you might be able to recognize that you've had since childhood.

_____

_____

_____

_____

_____

Remember:

● Childhood healing fantasies are coping mechanisms created in response to an emotionally immature parent to maintain hope through a difficult childhood.

● Recognizing and letting go of these fantasies allows you to choose an authentic path forward.

● Childhood healing fantasies can be uncovered by reflecting on the goals that you've been pursuing based on your parent's, family's, or society's expectations, and identifying any associated "should," "have to," or "must" thoughts.

43 Letting Go of Your Healing Fantasies, Part 2

FINALLY LEAVING HOME

Now THAT YOU'VE IDENTIFIED YOUR childhood healing fantasies, it's time to let them go and free yourself from the constraints they've placed on your life. This activity will guide you in releasing these fantasies and focusing on your authentic self, separate from the expectations and patterns associated with your emotionally immature parent. This activity will also help you create a healthier, more fulfilling life.

Here's HOW To let go of your childhood healing fantasies, shift your focus toward your own growth, healing, and self-discovery. Acknowledge the fantasies as a coping mechanism from your past and consciously release them, understanding that they no longer serve you. Embrace the idea that true healing comes from within and not from external achievements or validation.

Put It Into PRACTICE

1. Reflect on your healing fantasies by writing down the childhood healing fantasies you identified in the previous activity and the ways they have impacted your life, both positively and negatively.

2. Release these fantasies by creating a symbolic gesture or ritual to let go, such as writing them down and then safely burning or tearing the paper or sending it out to sea.

3. Replace these fantasies by creating new, healthier beliefs that are aligned with your true self, focusing on personal growth, resilience, and self-compassion. For example:

- Old fantasy: "If I achieve career success and become wealthy, my emotionally immature parent will finally be proud of me and provide the love and validation that I've always longed for."

- New, healthier belief: "My self-worth and happiness come from within without needing external achievements or my parent's approval. I deserve love and validation for who I am, not just for what I accomplish."

4. Set realistic authentic goals that reflect your values and desires, rather than those based on your parent's or society's expectations. For example, your parent's expectation could be for you to become a doctor, dentist, lawyer, engineer, etc. because it is a prestigious career and will bring financial security. Your realistic authentic goal could be to pursue a career in art or graphic design because it aligns with your passion for creativity, self-expression, and desire to make a positive impact through visual art.

Remember:

- Even if your healing fantasy comes true one day, it won't heal you or your parent's problems. It won't undo the past.

- To really heal, let go of the fantasy and choose to live a life that's true to who you are now.

- Set realistic goals that are based on your wants and needs—not someone else's.

44 Forgiving Yourself

RELEASING THE PAST TO BE FREE TODAY

FORGIVENESS IS A CRITICAL PART of healing from your past, letting go of painful childhood memories and experiences, and experiencing joy today. You can blame and shame yourself for what happened in the past. For example, you may ruminate over past mistakes and failures, negatively compare yourself to others, exaggerate your flaws, belittle your accomplishments, engage in negative self-talk, and/or hold on to unrealistic perfectionistic standards. This isn't helpful for you to heal and move forward. You can't change the past. You didn't know what you know now, and now that you know better you can try and *do* better in the future.

Instead, choose to forgive yourself. Choose to accept what happened even if it was painful and wrong, and become accountable for healing and making sure you don't repeat the same mistakes in the future.

Here's HOW In this activity, you'll practice forgiving yourself by identifying a painful memory that you're still holding on to, gaining clarity of how you might still be punishing yourself for the wrongs of the past, and creating a new relationship of self-acceptance.

Put It Into PRACTICE

1. Think of a past memory that you may regret involving your parent. What was it that you might've done or said (or didn't do or say) that you regret? What happened?

_____

_____

2. Are you still punishing yourself for what happened? If so, how are you still punishing yourself for what happened? For example, isolating yourself, engaging in unhealthy relationships, neglecting self-care, working too much, abusing substances, or rejecting help.

_____

_____

_____

_____

_____

3. The guilt, shame, and blame you may be carrying isn't going to change what happened. Holding on to this pain isn't going to undo what happened either. It's only causing unnecessary pain for yourself. You've held on to it long enough; it's time to release the burden. Write out your forgiveness to yourself. Begin with "I forgive myself for…" You can return to this whenever you catch yourself feeling bad about yourself for what happened in the past. Repeat it often as an affirmation.

_____

_____

_____

_____

_____

Remember:

- Regretful things happen. You didn't know what you know now.

- Forgiving yourself means forgiving what you might've done in the past and letting go of punishing, neglecting, or self-sabotaging your happiness today.

- In forgiving yourself, you can face the future with accountability for what you will not do or say again.

45 Forgiving Your Parent

A GUIDED MEDITATION FOR BEING HAPPY TODAY.

IT CAN BE HARD TO forgive an emotionally immature parent for how they impacted your childhood and adult life. You might have so much anger, bitterness, and resentment toward them for what they did and said, and for what they didn't do and say. You may want them to admit what they did and said, confess that they were wrong, apologize, change, and possibly even be punished for what happened. But forgiving them doesn't need to be about them. It doesn't need to be about punishing them or getting an apology from them. It can be about reclaiming your happiness.

Here's HOW You can't change the past or control how your parent behaves. It is out of your control whether they get punished for what they did, realize what they did was wrong, apologize, or choose to change. What you can control is whether you go into the future with the heavy weight of angry, hurt, and resentful feelings or with a focus on finding your own joy.

Put It Into PRACTICE In this activity, you'll practice reclaiming your happiness through the guided meditation provided at EmotionallyImmatureParents.com. If you don't want to practice the guided meditation or don't have access to the website, you can think back to a memory involving your parent that brings up feelings of anger, resentment, hurt, injustice, and/or unfairness. Then reflect on these questions:

1. What happened that you continue to feel angry or resentful about?

_____

_____

_____

_____

_____

_____

_____

_____

2. Are you still wanting to punish your parent for this? If so, how are you trying to punish them (e.g., the silent treatment)?

_____

_____

_____

_____

_____

_____

_____

_____

3. Are you directly or indirectly punishing others or neglecting others in your adult life for what happened with your parent? For example, shutting down or avoiding them rather than listening to and providing what the other person needs.

_____

_____

_____

_____

_____

_____

_____

4. To remind yourself to let it go when you catch yourself dwelling in those painful memories and they are bringing up anger and resentment, repeat this forgiveness affirmation while visualizing your parent or whomever you want to forgive: "I forgive you; you forgive me. Let's live in love, peace, and harmony."

Remember:

- Forgiving your parent doesn't require them to finally apologize, own up to their mistakes, and change—otherwise you may be waiting forever to move forward.

- Forgiveness is for yourself, so you can let go of the past and be happy today and for the rest of your days.

- Forgive yourself and others so that you can live in love, peace, and harmony.

CHAPTER 9

Coming Home to the Present

The Power of Vulnerability and Trust

Vulnerability (courageously exposing your inside world) and trust (the belief in your own abilities, instincts, and judgments, or the abilities, instincts, and judgments of others) are crucial for personal growth and emotional well-being. They allow for authentic self-expression and help you cultivate deep, intimate connections with others. Embracing vulnerability especially enables you to build resilience, adaptability, and self-compassion—leading to a more fulfilling and meaningful life. In this chapter, you'll learn how to create more mutual respect, joy, and intimacy within your relationships through vulnerability and trust. You'll set realistic expectations, ask for what you want and what you need, and find power in showing the world who you are. You'll learn how to be yourself and let others in while navigating through your fears and insecurities.

46 Deepening Relationships

INTIMACY THROUGH VULNERABILITY

BEING VULNERABLE AND REVEALING YOUR inside world to others can feel scary. You might've been met with judgment, rejection, criticism, abandonment, and dismissal from your parent when you were vulnerable or shared your feelings with them. So today, you might have the same fears of rejection, judgment, and abandonment in your adult relationships. However, vulnerability and openness are how trust and intimacy are created. They are how you get to deeper levels of friendship, romance, and more. If you want to experience deep and intimate relationships, you'll have to face those fears and practice being vulnerable in your relationships.

Here's HOW You've been developing self-awareness and connecting with your true, authentic self. Now you can take the first step in vulnerability by expressing that self on the page. Not everyone will understand you, and that's okay; as long as you understand yourself and express who you are in a genuine way, you will open the door to deeper relationships.

Put It Into PRACTICE

1. Think of a relationship where you haven't been honest with yourself and the other person about how you're truly feeling, what your true thoughts are, what you want, etc.

   _____

   _____

   _____

   _____

2. What's been happening? What specifically doesn't feel true to you? (For example, maybe you agreed with them in the moment, but realized you actually don't agree. Or maybe they treated a service worker unkindly and it's bothering you.)

_____

_____

_____

_____

_____

3. How does this situation make you feel? What feelings have been coming up?

_____

_____

_____

_____

_____

4. What's not okay about this situation? What is it that makes you feel uncomfortable? Unsafe? Disrespected? (For example, they make plans for you both without asking what you want to do.)

_____

_____

_____

_____

_____

5. What do you need instead? Be as specific as possible. For example, to feel safe, respected, heard, and seen—"I need you to call me and ask before coming over"; "I need you to respond to my text message in two days, or let me know when you'll get back to me."

_____

_____

_____

_____

_____

_____

_____

_____

The challenge for you now is to take what you've identified previously and share it with the other person. In the next activity, I will share with you a vulnerable conversation framework to do just this.

Remember:

- It is through vulnerability that you build trust and true intimacy.

- Writing out your thoughts and feelings can help open the door to deeper connections.

- You can learn a lot about yourself by reflecting on a relationship where you haven't been honest with yourself or someone else.

Building Communication

THE POWER OF VULNERABILITY

THE WORDS YOU SAY MATTER. They can explain the emotions you feel to the other person and open up a sense of vulnerability that makes your relationship more intimate. The other person can also be inspired to be vulnerable in return. Don't expect that you'll be perfect in communicating vulnerably from the start, of course—just try your best. Vulnerability will get easier with practice as you become more confident, resilient, and experienced.

Here's HOW The vulnerable confrontation framework can help you communicate in a more vulnerable way. You can share your answer to each question with the other person to get to the heart of how you feel, how they feel, and where to go from here:

1. What did you see and hear in this situation? Be as specific and objective as possible. For example, "Mom, I saw that you called me six times earlier today."

2. How did what you see and hear make you feel? For example, "I know you didn't mean this, but it makes me feel anxious and overwhelmed to see all those missed calls when it's not an emergency."

3. What is your interpretation of this situation—the storyline in your head? For example, "The storyline in my head is that you're not respecting my time and you're not thinking about the stress that I'm in."

4. What do you want? What do you need? For example, "Next time, if I don't answer your first call, I will get back to you when I have time within 24 hours."

Put It Into PRACTICE Think of a recent situation you haven't addressed, and craft your message to the other person using the vulnerable conversation framework. You can share this message now, or use it as practice for using this framework when something comes up in the future.

Remember:

- Your words are powerful; choose them lovingly and kindly.

- Having a framework will make it easier for you to practice being vulnerable, whether you are showing appreciation for what someone's doing or talking about something they did that hurt you.

- Vulnerability becomes easier over time as you have more of these conversations and face the feelings that show up.

- Being vulnerable can feel scary, but it is part of creating genuine and intimate relationships.

- Your past rejections, abandonments, and emotional history might be showing up today in your fears of being vulnerable.

- There is no guarantee that others will meet you with acceptance and understand when you're being vulnerable, but that's a risk we all take to be true to ourselves.

48 Building Trust from Within

BRAVING

As IMPORTANT AS IT IS to be able to trust those close to you, it's arguably more important to be able to trust yourself. Self-trust is what will guide you in making decisions for yourself and expressing who you are, regardless of what others say. It is crucial in becoming an independent adult.

Here's HOW BRAVING is an acronym described by professor and author Brené Brown in an episode of her podcast where she talks about building trust within relationships. BRAVING stands for boundaries, reliability, accountability, vault, integrity, nonjudgment, and generosity. To have trust in yourself, you need to:

1. Have **boundaries**. Respect your own boundaries, let others know your boundaries, and be firm with others when it comes to your boundaries if you want to trust yourself.

2. Be **reliable**. Take care of and show up for yourself even when you don't want to.

3. Be **accountable**. Take ownership for the results of your actions.

4. Be a **vault**. Be the keeper of your own secrets, and only share personal information with people who have earned your trust.

5. Have **integrity**. Demonstrate your core values, mean what you say, and say what you mean. Behave according to your values even when no one is watching.

6. Be **nonjudgmental**. Accept yourself as you are.

7. Have **generosity**. Give yourself grace and the benefit of the doubt. Be gentle and kind with yourself when you make a mistake, when you're feeling down, when you're feeling scared, etc.

Put It Into PRACTICE   You're to go through each element of BRAVING and see where you can make changes and adjustments to build up self-trust:

1. Are there personal boundaries that you need to have to trust yourself more? For example, "I won't share personal information with people I don't really know." (You can turn to Chapter 10 for more information on boundaries to help you answer this question.)

2. Are there relationships and areas in your life where you can be more reliable and consistent? For example, to consistently show up on time or give a heads-up if you are running late? Are there relationships where you would need *them* to be more reliable and consistent? For example, for them to show up on time or give you a heads-up if they're running late?

3. Are you accountable to the results of your actions and inactions? Is there someone who can be your accountability partner, helping you track your accountability and brainstorm areas where you can be more accountable?

4. Do you tend to overshare? Maybe by giving personal details to people who haven't earned your trust? Or gossiping about things that you shouldn't have? Instead of oversharing, what can you talk about?

5. Are there particular relationships or roles where you don't match your words with your actions? Areas where you aren't sticking to your values?

6. Where in your life can you be more accepting of yourself?

7. Where in your life can you be gentler and kinder with yourself? What kind things can you say when you are feeling bad about yourself?

Remember:

- You can use BRAVING to build self-trust.
- BRAVING stands for boundaries, reliability, accountability, vault, integrity, nonjudgment, and generosity.
- Self-trust is key in being an independent adult and staying true to who you are.

49 Knowing Who's Trustworthy

THE POWER OF DISCERNMENT

SOMETIMES YOUR GUT FEELINGS ARE more accurate than your thoughts. Sometimes your thoughts are more accurate than your current feelings. As you work on building trust and being vulnerable in your relationships, you'll be using both to discern who is trustworthy and whether there's mutual trust in the relationship.

Here's HOW In the previous activity, you used BRAVING to develop self-trust. You can use the same method when discerning whether someone else is worthy of your trust as well. In the following practice, you will reflect on a specific relationship, answering with both your gut feelings and inner thoughts.

Put It Into PRACTICE

1. **Boundaries:** Does this person have healthy boundaries? Do they respect your boundaries when you tell them to?

2. **Reliability:** Do they show up for you most of the time? (Nobody is perfect; as long as they're mostly showing up the majority of the time, it is good enough.)

3. **Accountability:** Do they take ownership for their behaviors? Do they apologize and make amends when they're wrong or have accidentally done harm? Do they try to change and improve?

4. **Vault:** Do they keep your secrets? Have they told others about something personal that you told them, even if you were specific with letting them know not to tell others?

5. **Integrity:** Are they honest and do they live by their values? Are they who they say they are? Do their words match their actions and their actions with their words?

6. **Nonjudgment:** Are they accepting of you? Do you feel judged being around them? Are they understanding? Do they try to understand you?

7. **Generosity:** Do they give you grace and the benefit of the doubt? Do they accept apologies easily and move forward without holding grudges or having unspoken resentments?

8. What do your gut feelings tell you about whether this person is trustworthy or not?

Creating and building trust takes time, and not everyone that you meet is trustworthy. You have the power of discernment within you to know whether to trust someone.

Remember:

● Your thinking brain and your feeling body can help you discern if someone is trustworthy or not.

● Building trust in a relationship takes time, experience, and both parties working together to deserve each other's trust.

● BRAVING can help you reflect on the relationship more objectively and decide what needs to improve in order to nurture trust.

50 Identifying Needs and Wants

THE THREE-POINT AUTHENTIC CHECK-IN

WHEN IT COMES TO YOUR needs, psychologist Abraham Maslow created the hierarchy of needs. Starting at the bottom of this pyramid diagram are your physiological needs (basic survival needs, like water and food), next are safety needs (shelter, security), then love and belonging, esteem (respect, freedom), and finally self-actualization (enlightenment or achieving your highest potential) sits at the top. Meanwhile, your wants are the desires that you have. They may bring more happiness to your life, whether temporary or longer lasting. There's nothing wrong with wanting things. If you lost your ability to want and desire, you would never get out of bed.

Your ability to know what you need may have been disrupted by early experiences of having your needs ignored or even rejected by an emotionally immature parent. Your ability to know what you want may have also been disrupted if you were made to feel guilty for wanting something.

Here's HOW If you struggle to understand your needs or wants, you can use a three-point authentic check-in to help. As frequently as you can throughout the day, take a short pause and do the following practice.

Put It Into PRACTICE

1. Close your eyes if you feel comfortable.

2. Place both hands on your chest or one hand on your chest and the other hand on your belly.

3. Take three deep inhales and exhales. Sigh loudly on each exhale.

4. Ask yourself these three questions:

   1. How am I feeling right now?

   2. What do I need right now?

   3. What do I want right now?

Initially, you may experience confusion and frustration. Keep asking. Keep checking in. Keep knocking and the door will eventually open and let you in.

Write down your observations.

_____

_____

_____

_____

_____

_____

_____

_____

_____

_____

Remember:

● Your needs are nonnegotiable; you need them to live and have a healthy life.

● Your wants and desires are what get you up in the morning.

● Your ability of needing and wanting might have been disrupted growing up with a parent who neglected or rejected your needs and made you feel guilty or greedy for wanting things.

● Regularly practicing the three-point authentic check-in can help you uncover your needs and wants.

51 | Living with Standards

IDENTIFYING WHAT YOU WILL NOT TOLERATE

YOUR PARENT MAY HAVE HAD low standards or no standards for what they allowed/tolerated from others. This is because emotionally immature parents tend to struggle with self-awareness, self-worth, and emotional regulation, leading to difficulties in setting healthy expectations for themselves and their relationships. Instead, they may have modeled to you to tolerate hurtful and disrespectful behaviors from others. Now you may end up repeating these same patterns in your adult relationships, tolerating hurtful and disrespectful behaviors from friends, significant others, and/or family.

You have the right to expect certain things in your relationships. You deserve to not tolerate, accept, or allow negative behaviors. Recognize your own standards, uphold them, and live by them.

Here's HOW Your standards are the level of quality acceptable for you. It's where you draw the line of what's okay and tolerable versus what's not okay and intolerable. When it comes to choosing adult relationships, you can then choose to be with people who meet your standards and spend less time or no time with people who don't. You are not being mean, rude, or superior by living with standards. You are holding people accountable for how they treat you.

Put It Into PRACTICE Your standards can be different across different relationships, and they can change as you grow and change. To reflect on your present standards, start by thinking about a relationship that you have, perhaps with one of your parents. Answer these questions with that relationship in mind:

1. What are my standards within this relationship? For example, "to be completely honest with each other even when we're scared of hurting each other's feelings."

_____

_____

2. What will I absolutely not tolerate in this relationship? For example, "this person talking poorly about me behind my back."

_____

_____

3. When was a time that they didn't meet your standards and you let it slide? What happened? How did this make you feel?

_____

_____

4. When was a time they did or said something that made you feel hurt and you tolerated it? What happened?

_____

_____

In the next exercise, you will dive deeper into living by your standards and also ensuring those standards are realistic. This is important prep work for setting healthy boundaries in Chapter 10.

Remember:

- Growing up, your parent may have modeled to you to tolerate hurtful and disrespectful behaviors.

- Choose to have standards; they are your right.

- Standards change over time. Revisit this activity as you grow to keep track of your standards.

52 Having Realistic Expectations
ADJUSTING YOUR STANDARDS

HAVING STANDARDS IS PART OF any healthy relationship. The problems arise when these expectations are either too high, too low, unspoken, and/or unrealistic. You don't want to have too high/unrealistic expectations because you may end up feeling disappointed. And too low of expectations (or no expectations) means that even though you may never be disappointed, you might create a self-fulfilling prophecy that nothing good will happen. You also don't want unspoken expectations because unless someone is a mind reader, they won't know what your expectations are.

Here's HOW As you are building trust with yourself and others and cultivating healthy relationships, you will need to keep your expectations realistic and communicate them directly. (You will learn more about communicating expectations in Activity 53: Asking for What You Want and Need.) Knowing each other's expectations gives clarity in the relationship rather than confusion, disappointment, frustration, and resentment. Knowing your own expectations and ensuring they are realistic help you maintain a balance between not setting yourself up for disappointment and not manifesting the worst outcomes.

Put It Into PRACTICE

1. Can you think of a time when you had high expectations and you ended up feeling disappointed because things didn't turn out the way you expected? What happened?

2. Can you think of a time when you had an unrealistic expectation of someone (e.g., that your parent would change overnight)? What was it? How did you feel when they didn't meet your expectation?

_____

_____

_____

3. Can you think of a time when you had low expectations and the situation turned out better than you expected? What happened?

_____

_____

_____

4. When it comes to your parent, what are realistic expectations that you can have for them and your interactions with them? For example, "I expect that it'll be uncomfortable setting boundaries with my parent, and I might stumble over my words or lose control of my emotions."

_____

_____

_____

Remember:

- It's normal to have expectations.

- High or unrealistic expectations can lead to constant disappointment, while low expectations can invite a self-fulfilling prophecy of nothing turning out well.

- Exploring your expectations can help you identify where they are too high, unrealistic, too low, or nonexistent.

53 Asking for What You Want and Need

A GUIDED MEDITATION ON THE POWER OF ASKING

REMEMBER THAT ONE OF THE fifteen rights to live by is that you have the right to stand up for yourself (see Activity 25: Becoming Emotionally Mature). You may find it difficult to ask for what you want and what you need for several reasons. One may be your early experiences with your emotionally immature parent and watching how they interacted with other adults. Because they were unable to model a healthy communication of needs and wants and also might have reacted negatively to your needs and wants, you might feel selfish for asking for what you want and need now. You might feel like a burden for bothering the other person. You may be afraid of being rejected for asking, upsetting, or angering them and being punished. You have the right to ask. It doesn't mean they have to oblige—maybe they are busy or unavailable or just don't want to. But you are not selfish or a burden for asking. Ask, and maybe they will willingly say yes. It might even bring them joy to say yes to you.

Here's HOW Practice asking in low-stress situations where the requests are small and within relationships you feel comfortable and safe in. Get familiar with the uncomfortable emotions that show up as you're thinking about asking them, as you're asking them, and afterward. This practice will help you feel more prepared and ready as you start asking for the larger things you want and need in higher-stress situations like one with your parent.

Put It Into PRACTICE In this practice, you will move through difficult emotions of asking for what you want and need with the guided meditation provided at EmotionallyImmatureParents.com. If you don't want to practice the guided meditation or don't have access to the website, you can instead go through the following steps:

1. Think of a specific situation where you need to ask for something you want or need, be it big or small. Write down the details of the situation, including who is involved and what you hope to achieve.

2. Is there any resistance you may have to asking for what you want in this situation? Write down the fears, beliefs, or other factors that may be holding you back, and acknowledge them without judgment.

3. Repeat these affirmations or create your own to repeat ("I have the right to ask for what I want and need." "My needs and desires are important." "I am worthy of receiving what I ask for."). Repeat them to yourself out loud as many times as you need until you feel more empowered and confident.

4. Write out a plan for how you will ask for what you want or need. Write down the specific steps you will take, along with any obstacles you may need to overcome.

5. Seek out support and encouragement by telling someone you trust about your plan before you go through with it.

6. After implementing your plan, take a moment to reflect on the outcome. What did you learn from the experience? How can you apply this newfound confidence and assertiveness to other areas of your life?

Remember:

- You have the right to ask, and they have the right to answer as they wish.

- When people say no to your ask, they're not rejecting you.

- You can always ask why if they say no to your ask. You may be surprised at their reason.

- Your confidence will build as you move through challenging situations and your fears of asking for what you want and need.

54 Cultivating Genuine Relationships

LETTING YOUR WALLS FALL AND EXPOSING YOUR BEAUTIFUL HEART

YOU HAVE A BEAUTIFUL HEART. You might've had experiences in the past with your parent, other family members, a friend, or significant other where you exposed your heart and they didn't take good care of it. You might've learned from these experiences to guard and protect your hurt heart. You might've even become quite comfortable with having your guard up in old and new relationships, closing off your heart to avoid more hurt. However, depth and intimacy in any relationship will require you to open again and reveal your heart once more. This is a risk that you must take to truly be loved for who you are and let yourself truly love others.

Here's HOW Bringing your awareness from your head down to your heart and becoming sensitive to both bodily sensations around the chest and feelings coming from the heart will guide you to become more openhearted. Creating an affirmation to remind yourself to stay openhearted throughout the day will also help as you train yourself to give and receive love.

Put It Into PRACTICE

1. Place two hands over your heart.

2. Imagine bringing the focus of your attention from your head down, down, down toward your chest.

3. Notice the pressure of your hands against your chest.

4. Now imagine bringing the spotlight of your attention through the front of your chest, beyond your front ribs, into the core of your chest where your heart resides.

5. Be here in the home of your heart, noticing passing breaths, feeling your chest expanding and contracting, and noticing what other sensations show up.

6. Whisper to yourself (from your heart): "Stay open; don't fight it. You're so loving. You're so loved."

7. Repeat this affirmation as many times as you need until you feel more open.

8. Return to this affirmation throughout your day—and moving forward.

9. Be patient with yourself and this process of opening your heart and letting your defenses fall. Embrace the push and pull of your opening and closing.

You may feel scared exposing your heart, but you might also experience a feeling of relief, freedom, and power when you are vulnerable in this way. You might even inspire others to be more open as well.

Remember:

● Negative experiences from the past might have taught you to guard your heart.

● Closing your heart stops you from truly loving yourself and others and blocks you from receiving love.

● Experiencing deep and intimate relationships will require you to expose your heart once more.

55 Cultivating Safe and Respectful Relationships

A GUIDED MEDITATION IN SHARING YOUR INSECURITIES

YOU MIGHT'VE NOT FELT SAFE and respected growing up in your home and possibly still feel unsafe and disrespected with your parent. They might be lacking empathy, communication skills, and active listening abilities to understand your insecurities and make you feel safe and respected. Knowing what makes you feel insecure and then asking and consistently reminding the other person of these things will help you create safety and respect in your relationships. Remember that you have the right to teach people how best to show up for you and your unique insecurities, but they get to choose if they'll meet you there. They get to choose if they'll respect your insecurities (even if they don't understand why you might feel insecure about something) and whether they will help you feel more secure in the relationship.

Here's HOW First, gain clarity by writing out what specific behaviors in a relationship make you feel secure and what behaviors make you feel insecure. Examples of what can make you feel secure are: consistent and reliable support from loved ones, a stable living environment, effective communication skills, and a strong sense of self-worth and self-esteem. Examples of what can make you feel insecure include: inconsistent or unreliable support from loved ones, an unstable or chaotic living environment, poor communication skills, and low self-worth and self-esteem. Remember, every person is unique, and we all have our differences—what makes you insecure can be different from what makes someone else insecure. These differences are okay; you can learn to respect and show up for them as they need it and not when you think that they need it.

Put It Into PRACTICE In this practice, you will develop courage and confidence to talk to others about your insecurities by following the guided meditation provided at EmotionallyImmatureParents .com. If you don't want to practice the guided meditation or don't have access to the website, you can instead follow these steps:

1. Think of a specific relationship, and write out specific behaviors that they're either doing or not doing that make you feel secure.

2. Now write out behaviors they are either doing or not doing that make you feel insecure.

3. Using what you uncovered in steps 1 and 2, ask for what you need in order to feel secure, and tell them what makes you feel insecure.

4. Regularly remind them of your securities and insecurities, and give them positive reinforcement when they show up for you in a way that makes you feel secure. For example, you can express gratitude to them by saying something like, "Thanks for taking the time to listen to me. This makes me feel really seen and understood." Or by offering them encouragement and praise, saying something like, "I really appreciate how you've been making an effort to communicate more openly with me. I feel a stronger connection between us."

Remember:

- Everyone has their own insecurities, so what makes you feel secure can be different from what makes someone else feel secure.

- You have the right to ask for security and communicate what makes you feel insecure.

- Just because you ask doesn't mean that the other person will show up for you and try to act on what makes you feel secure.

- Get to know exactly what makes you secure in a relationship and what makes you feel insecure. Then clearly communicate this to the other person.

56 Navigating Through Your Fears

LETTING OTHERS IN

IT'S OKAY—IT'S HUMAN—TO FEEL SCARED. What matters is that you don't let your fears keep you from growing. The things that scare you also point you toward healing and growth. Your fears offer opportunities to practice being vulnerable, asking for what you want and need, building trust, and so much more. Your journey to recovery as a child of an emotionally immature parent will require you to become fearless. Please keep in mind here that being fearless doesn't mean never experiencing fear again. Being fearless means that in spite of feeling fear, you choose to act in a way that will help you heal and grow.

Here's HOW Becoming aware of what you are afraid of and talking to others about these fears will help you grow and heal through them. As tempting as it may be to avoid the fear, getting familiar with it, allowing yourself to feel it, and letting others in on what you feel are helpful to your journey.

Put It Into PRACTICE What are you most afraid of in your relationships? Look through the list of common fears and reflect on the following questions:

- Being abandoned.
- Being rejected.
- Being judged.
- Being a burden.
- Not being good enough.

- Not living up to expectations.
- Making a mistake.
- Disappointing them.
- Upsetting or angering them.

1. What fears in this list resonate with you?

_____

_____

_____

2. Are there other fears that come up for you?

_____

_____

_____

3. How have these fears been negatively impacting you, other people, and your relationships?

_____

_____

_____

4. How do you typically tend to react out of your fears?

_____

_____

_____

5. What if you saw your fears as opportunities to grow and heal? How might you approach your relationships differently?

_____

_____

_____

6. How can you talk to your loved ones about your fears and what scares you the most? Draft what you will say, and be sure to ask that you have them on your side as you navigate through your fears.

_____

_____

_____

_____

_____

_____

_____

_____

_____

_____

Remember:

- Your fear is a gateway to growth and healing.

- Being fearless isn't about having no fear. Being fearless means that in spite of your fear, you choose what you need and want.

- Identifying your fears, getting comfortable with feeling fear, and talking to others about your fears are how you grow, heal, and practice fearlessness.

CHAPTER 10

Firm and Healthy Boundaries

Why They Are Needed for You to Heal, Be Authentic, and Be Free

You learned a bit about the importance of boundaries in Part 1 and the signs that you need boundaries. Now it's time to look deeper into the boundaries you may be lacking and take steps toward setting (and maintaining) those boundaries. In this chapter, you will learn about the seven different types of boundaries, communication strategies, and a powerful framework for setting and sticking with your boundaries when others react negatively. You'll use the boundary circle tool to gain clarity on what's going on inside your relationship right now that's not okay and practice the 7-38-55 rule of effective communication so you can have better results when you talk with your parent and other emotionally immature adults.

57 Exploring the Seven Types of Boundaries

WHAT YOU MUST PROTECT

THERE ARE SEVEN DIFFERENT TYPES of boundaries revolving around seven different areas in your life. These are:

1. **Physical boundaries:** Who's allowed to touch you and whether you want to touch them, and how others talk about your body.

2. **Material boundaries:** Who you lend your stuff to, what you're willing to let others borrow, what the terms and conditions of borrowing your belongings are, and what happens if they lose or damage it.

3. **Time boundaries:** Whether you let others use some of your time, how they are to use it, and for how long.

4. **Sexual boundaries:** What's too soon or not as soon as you want when it comes to sex, what you like and don't like, what turns you on and what turns you off, and what you find inappropriate to do or say.

5. **Emotional boundaries:** Feeling your feelings, taking as long as you need to process difficult emotions, and letting others know when you're feeling hurt, scared, uncomfortable, anxious, etc.

6. **Mental boundaries:** Thinking what you think, freely expressing your thoughts, deciding what topics you don't want to talk about, sharing personal information (or not), and agreeing to disagree.

7. **Religious/spiritual boundaries:** What you believe in.

Here's HOW You have the right to set boundaries revolving around these seven areas of your life. What types of boundaries might you be lacking right now?

Put It Into
PRACTICE

1. Can you identify a time when someone violated these boundaries?

_____

_____

2. Which types of boundaries are you more comfortable with setting? Why? Which types of boundaries are you most uncomfortable with setting? Why?

_____

_____

_____

3. Who do you struggle setting boundaries with?

_____

_____

4. Can you identify a time when you might've violated someone else's boundaries? What different types of boundaries have you violated?

_____

_____

Now that you understand the different domains in your life that you have the right to protect and set boundaries around, it'll be up to you to set these boundaries when needed and maintain them. You will practice these steps later in this chapter.

Remember:

- The seven types of boundaries are physical, material, time, sexual, emotional, mental, and religious/spiritual.

- Some boundaries can feel easier or more difficult to set than others.

- Sometimes you may violate someone else's boundaries. It happened; learn from this experience.

58 Being Gentle with Yourself

A GUIDED MEDITATION FOR PREPARING TO SET HEALTHY BOUNDARIES

BOUNDARIES ARE HOW YOU LET others know what makes you uncomfortable and how you ask for what you want and need. However, boundaries get especially confusing and emotional between you and your parent, as they may have never been healthy, firm, established, and respected in the past. This leads to difficulties in setting boundaries with your parent (and others) now. To set yourself up for success when setting boundaries, it is helpful to first do some work that builds confidence and self-trust.

Here's HOW Repetition of ideas can help ingrain these ideas in your mind. This is why positive affirmations, or repeated inspirational phrases, can be so helpful when working with beliefs that have been drilled into you over time and can build confidence when self-doubt is a challenge for you.

Put It Into PRACTICE In this practice, you will start using affirmations by following the guided meditation provided at Emotionally ImmatureParents.com. Then you will answer the questions that follow to reflect on the activity. If you don't want to practice the guided meditation or don't have access to the website, you can instead repeat these positive affirmations ten times:

- May I tune into my true, authentic self.

- May I be kind to myself through this challenging process.

- May I be patient with myself as I'm learning what's valuable to me.

1. After repeating the affirmations, say them one more time, slowly, while visualizing offering forgiveness and understanding to yourself. Feel a sense of inner strength and self-compassion as you do.

2. Write out these affirmations and put them where you will see them often, like above your desk, around a mirror, etc.

3. Remind yourself of your affirmations often, either saying them in your mind or out loud.

Choose to be kind to yourself, just as you would when talking to a loved one. Setting boundaries and even thinking about setting boundaries with your parent can bring up intense, uncomfortable feelings and thoughts. But you aren't being selfish for choosing to take care of yourself.

REFLECTION QUESTIONS

1. In what ways can I live like my authentic self?

2. How can I be patient with myself as I take steps toward setting boundaries with my parent?

3. How have I not been kind with myself in the past when facing a difficult situation?

Remember:

● Setting boundaries and even thinking about setting boundaries with your parent can bring up intense, uncomfortable feelings and even negative thoughts.

● Choose to be kind to yourself, with the same kindness you would use when talking to a loved one.

● Positive affirmations can help ingrain the ideas of self-confidence and self-kindness in your mind.

59 Reframing Your View of Boundaries

A FENCE WITH A GATE AND AN INVITATION

WHEN IT COMES TO SETTING boundaries with your parent and other adults in your life, it's not just about saying no, turning down their requests, or calling out their hurtful behaviors and repeating issues. It's also about what you're saying yes to, asking others for requests and favors, and inviting in respectful, loving, and supportive behaviors. One way of conceptualizing boundaries to help you keep this balance in mind as you set your own boundaries is through the fence and gate model.

Here's HOW Imagine that you are surrounded by a protective fence with a gate that opens to the good and closes to the bad. What comes to mind as bad? What do you want to invite in? Use this visualization as you set boundaries to help identify what you want and need—and what you don't want or need.

Put It Into PRACTICE The following circle represents you in the center and the protective fence and gate—your boundaries— surrounding you. If you aren't using a physical copy of this book, or don't wish to write in the book itself, you can copy this circle onto a blank piece of paper for the following steps.

1. Write or draw on the inside of the circle what makes you feel loved, seen, heard, respected, supported, and comfortable within your relationships (e.g., hugs, when people show up on time).

2. Write or draw outside of the circle what makes you feel unloved, unseen, unheard, disrespected, unsupported, and uncomfortable within your relationships (e.g., yelling, name-calling, the silent treatment).

Boundary Circle

Building and maintaining both your fence and gate—especially with your parent—will likely bring up uncomfortable feelings. Keep in mind as you continue through this journey and the next activities that you are only responsible for your actions and how you express your boundaries, not what others may think, do, or say about them. You are not shutting out the good; you are preventing the bad from entering.

Remember:

- Setting boundaries includes saying no to the things you don't need or want.

- Setting boundaries also includes saying yes to and welcoming the things that you want and need.

- Imagining boundaries through the fence and gate model can help you keep the balance of good and bad in mind while setting boundaries.

- You are not shutting out the good; you are preventing the bad from entering.

60 Building Up the Good and Keeping Out the Bad

CONTINUING THE BOUNDARY CIRCLE

YOUR PARENT MIGHT HAVE BEEN your biggest boundary buster growing up—and they may still be today. There are several reasons why your parent might struggle with respecting your boundaries:

1. **Lack of self-awareness:** They may not recognize their own needs for boundaries, making it difficult for them to understand and respect yours. For example, your parent might not understand your need for privacy and personal space, so they might show up to your place unannounced or go through your personal belongings.

2. **Need for control:** They may struggle with the idea of losing control and influence over you. For example, they might insist on managing your finances, making decisions about your career, or even dictating your choice of friends or romantic partners.

3. **Need for validation:** They may have an excessive need for emotional support and validation. For example, they might expect you to constantly comfort them or prioritize their emotional needs over yours, even in situations where it's inappropriate or burdensome for you.

4. **Inability to adapt:** They might be having difficulties adjusting to the changing relationship dynamics with you as you're growing up and developing independence. For example, they might insist on being involved in every aspect of your life, from daily decision-making to personal matters, without recognizing that you need the freedom and autonomy to make your own choices.

5. **Fear of abandonment:** They might fear losing connection with you as you're becoming more independent, forming new relationships, and/ or creating your own life. So they might be violating your boundaries to keep you close. For example, they might frequently call or text you and expect an immediate response or constant communication.

6. **Unresolved emotional issues:** They may be projecting their own unresolved emotional issues, such as unmet emotional needs, unprocessed trauma, or unhealthy family dynamics, onto you, causing them to blur boundaries in an attempt to address their own issues. For example, if they experienced neglect or emotional distance from their own parents, they might seek emotional closeness with you to heal that past wound.

Of course, with all the complex feelings involved in this relationship, you may be confused or even doubtful about what is okay, what isn't okay, and whether you actually need a boundary. The boundary circle you filled out in the previous activity can help you gain clarity.

Here's HOW Now that you have filled out a boundary circle with the things that make you feel safe, comfortable, seen, heard, supported, and respected—and the things that make you feel unsafe, uncomfortable, unseen, unheard, unsupported, and disrespected—you can get more specific. What do you enjoy and want to invite into your relationship with your parent? What do you want to limit in this relationship?

Put It Into PRACTICE Using your previous boundary circle as a guide, fill in the provided circle (or a new circle on a blank piece of paper) with things that are specific to your relationship with your parent. Ask yourself:

- What are they currently doing or saying that goes inside the circle?

- What are they currently doing or saying that goes outside the circle?

- Is there anything that's missing from inside the circle that would make you feel safer, more loved, supported, and respected?

- Is there anything that they're not doing or not saying that makes you feel unsafe, unsupported, unloved, or disrespected?

You may want to make a boundary circle for each of your important relationships eventually, especially if you are feeling unsure of where to start setting boundaries in those other relationships.

Remember:

- A boundary circle can help you gain clarity on what's going well in your relationships, what's happening that's not okay, and what's missing.

- You will need to create a different boundary circle for each of your relationships because each one is unique.

- People change. You may need to update your boundary circles as your relationships progress.

61 Setting Healthy Boundaries

SCRIPTS FOR EFFECTIVE COMMUNICATION

WHEN IT COMES TO SETTING boundaries, keeping this healthy boundary framework in mind can help to:

1. Gain clarity on the relationship and the boundaries that are needed.

2. Communicate the boundary.

3. Maintain the boundary and remind the other person of this boundary.

4. Change a boundary, negotiate the details of a boundary, and make exceptions to a boundary as needed.

You have already worked on step 1 previously in this chapter. Now it's time to take care of step 2. Sometimes communicating your boundaries can be quick, in the moment, and simple. Other times, it can require a back-and-forth discussion. It can also take time and effort for lasting positive changes to happen (see step 3). Regardless of what it takes to communicate a certain boundary, there are some simple scripts and guidelines you can follow to make sure you are sharing your limits with clarity and even compassion.

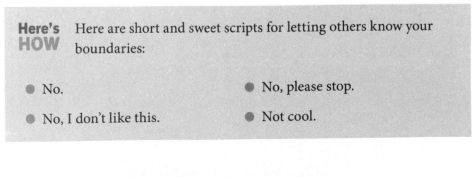

Here's HOW Here are short and sweet scripts for letting others know your boundaries:

- No.
- No, I don't like this.
- No, please stop.
- Not cool.

- This makes me feel bad.

- This makes me feel uncomfortable.

- I really don't like this. Stop.

- No, thanks.

- Like I said, I don't like this. Please stop.

The sooner the better; if you can, use one of these phrases to let the person know in the moment when they are doing or saying something that isn't okay with you. If you can't say something in the moment or don't recognize that what they're saying or doing is disrespectful, hurtful, or rude until later, let them know as soon as possible through text, a quick phone call, or the next time you see them in person.

If you've tried shorter scripts but are not getting the positive results you deserve, then the following bread-and-butter script can help get the message across. Use it to let your parent know in more detail how you're feeling, set a boundary, and ask for what you want or need instead:

"I feel _____ when you do or say (or don't do or don't say) _____ . Next time, I'd like for you to do or say (or not do or not say) _____ instead."

You can sprinkle in some empathy and love to show that this boundary comes from a compassionate place, like this:

"Hey Mom, there's something that's been bothering me. I know you don't mean to, but when you comment about my weight, it makes me feel really bad. I love you and I care about this relationship, and that's why I'm telling you this. Next time, I'd like it if you didn't talk about my weight. I'll remind you if you forget. Okay?"

Put It Into PRACTICE

1. Flip to a boundary circle that you created for one of your relationships. Take a look at what you wrote outside of the circle. What is it that they're doing or saying (or not doing or not saying) that's not okay?

_____

_____

2. The next time you are with them and they do this, what short script(s) can you use to communicate that you are not okay with that behavior?

_____

_____

3. Now imagine that they keep repeating this behavior after you told them to stop. How can you further explain your boundary using the bread-and-butter script?

_____

_____

4. Lastly, what can you add to the bread-and-butter script so that it sounds like you and is infused with more love and empathy?

_____

_____

5. Use what you've written to communicate your boundary to that person. You can practice first in relationships that you feel safe in and to build up your confidence before adapting the script in more challenging relationships, like with your parent.

    Remember:
    - Setting a boundary can be quick, short, and in the moment. "No" is a complete sentence.

    - Use the bread-and-butter script to let the person know how their action/comment is making you feel and what you'd like from them instead.

    - Infusing your words with love and empathy can make them easier to swallow.

62 | Speaking So They Want to Listen
THE 7-38-55 RULE

EFFECTIVELY COMMUNICATING IS CHALLENGING, BUT trying to effectively, calmly, *and* respectfully communicate with your parent can feel especially difficult. The 7-38-55 rule can help as you practice the scripts in the previous activity. It was created by Albert Mehrabian, a professor of psychology who wanted to understand the influence of nonverbal communication. This rule says that only 7 percent of what you get across to the other person consists of the actual words that you say. Thirty-eight percent of what gets communicated to them is in the volume and tonality of your voice, while most of what is communicated, the remaining 55 percent, depends on your body language.

Here's HOW Improving communication with your parent will require you to speak in a calm tone (if you can use a friendly tone, even better), have open and confident posture and calm facial expressions, and use nonaggressive gestures.

Put It Into PRACTICE

1. Think of a great speaker. Perhaps it's a celebrity, political or spiritual figure, motivational speaker, news anchor, etc.

   ● What does their voice sound like? Is it friendly? Is it loud? Is it monotone? Is it quiet?

   _____

   _____

   _____

- What do they do with their body as they speak? How is their posture? What facial expressions show up? What do they do with their hands and arms?

_____

_____

_____

_____

_____

2. Now reflect back to a time that you were having a difficult conversation, like a fight, disagreement, or an argument, with your parent.

- What was the tone of your voice like? How would someone listening in describe it?

_____

_____

_____

_____

_____

- What emotions were you experiencing?

_____

_____

_____

_____

_____

- How did those emotions show up in your body? What was your posture like? What were you doing with your hands and arms? What about your facial expression?

3. Practice speaking in front of a mirror and with people who you feel safe around, and practice being open and confident with your posture in everyday life.

4. The next time you have a difficult conversation with your parent, be mindful of the volume and tone of your voice. Try to emulate what you like about great speakers.

Remember:

- The 7-38-55 rule of communication describes that what gets communicated is 7 percent the words that you say, 38 percent the volume and tone of your voice, and 55 percent nonverbal body language.

- You can't make people want to listen to you, but you can increase the likelihood that they are willing to listen by improving your tonality and body language.

- You can practice your tone and body language in front of a mirror and/or with people who you feel safe around.

63 Handling Negative Reactions

A GUIDED MEDITATION IN STAYING THE COURSE

REMEMBER THAT SETTING BOUNDARIES AND letting others know your limits is a form of self-respect and self-care. You aren't being selfish for taking care of yourself. If something is not okay, it's your responsibility to be honest with yourself and let the other person know. However, their reaction is on them. Sometimes you may communicate as kindly and clearly as possible, but they still get upset or angry. That emotional response is their responsibility, so don't try to take it on as your own.

Here's HOW The common reactions that you might encounter when you communicate a boundary to your parent are in the following list. Going into the process of setting boundaries with these possible reactions in mind and being able to spot them in the moment as they're happening will be key to navigating through them while maintaining your boundaries:

1. Ignoring you.

2. Giving you the silent treatment.

3. Testing your limits (intentionally pushing or challenging your boundaries to see how you will react or how much you'll tolerate).

4. Asking for you to explain why you are doing this.

5. Trying to guilt-trip you.

6. Having an angry outburst.

7. Making threats (e.g., of leaving or ending the relationship, hurting themselves, withdrawing support, publicly shaming or criticizing you, or alienating you from the rest of the family).

8. Accepting your boundary.

Put It Into PRACTICE   In this practice, you will go through RAIN to rehearse a future situation where you handle your parent's negative reaction to a boundary you set. You can either follow the guided meditation provided at EmotionallyImmatureParents.com or walk through the steps of RAIN that follow:

1. Imagine a future situation where you need to set a boundary with someone in your life, perhaps an emotionally immature parent. Visualize the specific date, time, and place where you will set this boundary.

2. As you picture this person, say your boundary out loud or in your mind.

3. **R:** Recognize and notice inside your body what emotions and sensations are coming up. You might be feeling anxious, scared, or angry. You might be feeling your belly tightening, your throat constricting, and your heart beating faster.

4. **A:** Allow these feelings and sensations to be here. Don't judge them. Don't try to push them away. Whatever feeling(s) you have is okay.

5. **I:** Investigate with loving curiosity. Ask yourself: "Where is this feeling coming from?" "Have I felt this way before?" "How can I be with this?" "What do I need to move through this?" "What can I remind myself to help me make it through this?"

6. **N:** nurture. Tell yourself encouraging and supportive words, like, "I love you. We're going to make it through this. I won't leave you," "I'm here for you no matter what. This might feel uncomfortable, but I am up for the challenge," or "We got this! We've made it through similar uncomfortable situations before."

7. Carry the sense of strength and resilience that you have cultivated here with you as you continue to set healthy boundaries with your parent and others in your life, even in the face of negative reactions.

Write down your observations.

_____

_____

_____

_____

_____

_____

_____

_____

_____

_____

_____

_____

_____

Remember:

- Setting boundaries and letting others know your limitations is a form of self-care and self-respect.

- You're responsible for your own thoughts, feelings, words, and actions—not for how anyone else may act or react.

- Negative emotional reactions can often happen as a result of communicating a boundary.

- Prepare for this possibility, and stay firm in your boundary.

64 Maintaining Boundaries
SETTING CONSEQUENCES

THERE MAY BE TIMES WHEN your parent is unwilling to respect your boundaries, or they improve but not as fast as you would like. This is where consequences come in. Setting consequences isn't about forcing people to change, punishing them, or controlling them. It's about letting them know that you are serious about your boundaries and that their actions or inactions have consequences. When setting consequences effectively, it's about what you will do if they choose to do/say the thing you are not okay with. It may be uncomfortable for you and for them, and they may not like the consequences, but it's how you let go of taking responsibility over other people's choices and actions and give that responsibility back to them.

Here's HOW If you've tried setting boundaries with your parent, have consistently and firmly reminded them, and they're still violating your boundaries, then you can set consequences. Remember, you're not threatening to punish the other person, but you're letting them know ahead of time that the next time they choose to violate your boundaries, this is what will happen. Once you set the consequence, you will need to follow it up with action or the other person won't take you seriously. Choose your consequences before talking to your parent, and stay firm but kind in how you communicate them.

Put It Into PRACTICE Think of a situation where your boundaries were being violated and you'd already reminded the person consistently of those boundaries. If you're new to setting boundaries, you can imagine a future scenario where your parent is not respecting your boundaries.

1. What are consequences that you can set? For example, if your boundary is not allowing the person to raise their voice at you, your consequence could be ending the conversation and trying again later when they are calm.

    _____

    _____

2. What if they continue to violate your boundaries, even with this consequence? What's the next consequence that you can set? For example, if your parent cannot stop raising their voice to you when talking about a certain topic, your consequence could be that you will not discuss this topic with them anymore.

    _____

    _____

3. Practice what you will say to communicate these consequences. For example, "I told you that it makes me feel scared when you raise your voice and yell. The next time we're having a disagreement and you choose to yell, I'll have to stop the conversation and we can try again at a later time." Or "You're yelling again, Dad. We talked about this before. If we can't have a calm debate about politics, then I don't want to talk politics with you next time."

    _____

    _____

Remember:

- Setting consequences isn't about making others change, punishing them, or controlling them.

- Setting consequences means teaching someone that they're responsible for their actions and their actions have results.

- You can build on a consequence if the person continues to ignore your boundary, working your way up to larger consequences.

65 Adapting Your Boundaries

WHEN PEOPLE AND SITUATIONS CHANGE

THERE WILL BE TIMES WHEN you need to adjust or let go of one of your boundaries because you've changed, the other person has changed, and/or the situation has changed. There will also be times when you can make an exception around one of your boundaries. Here are examples of when it's healthy to change your boundaries:

- **You've changed:** As you grow, heal, and evolve, your needs and comfort levels may change, so you might need to reassess or adjust your boundaries accordingly.

- **They've changed:** As they grow, heal, and evolve, you might feel more comfortable around them; they've stopped certain problematic behaviors, so you might feel comfortable relaxing certain boundaries.

- **The situation has changed:** Life changes, such as moving, starting a new job, change in season, or experiencing a significant loss, may require you to reassess your boundaries to accommodate new situations or emotional needs.

- **Deepening trust:** As trust deepens in a relationship, you might feel comfortable relaxing certain boundaries and opening up for greater vulnerability, closeness, and intimacy.

- **Concerns:** If someone respectfully communicates their concerns or needs regarding your boundaries, it may be worth considering whether adjusting the boundary is appropriate while still prioritizing your own well-being.

- **Misunderstandings:** Sometimes, boundaries may have been misunderstood or misinterpreted by the other person. In these cases, renegotiating or clarifying the boundary can lead to better communication and mutual understanding.

- **Rare circumstances:** Sometimes, a friend or family member might be experiencing a catastrophe or an emergency. In these cases, you might be willing to make an exception and temporarily adjust one of your boundaries.

Here's HOW When it comes to setting healthy boundaries, there must be a level of flexibility, consistency, and also firmness. You don't want to be too bendable, and you don't want to be too rigid. There will be times in your relationships when you will need to adjust, renegotiate, or even relax one or more of your boundaries. Trust in your own judgment and your feelings to gauge whether or not making changes is the best route.

Put It Into
PRACTICE

1. Think of a relationship where you are currently not feeling as though your wants and needs are being met with the boundaries that have been set. Also consider relationships where things have changed.

2. What is the current boundary? What adjustments or exceptions do you feel are needed at this time?

3. Use the bread-and-butter script to communicate this change to your boundary.

Remember:

- Sometimes, changes in yourself, others, or circumstances will require you to reassess or adjust your boundaries.

- Be open to adjusting boundaries while maintaining consistency and prioritizing your well-being.

- Communicate openly and honestly. Initiate conversations about boundary adjustments, ensuring clear communication and mutual understanding.

CHAPTER 11

Moving Forward

Growing Independently, Cultivating Mutual Respect, and Upholding Accountability

Relationships take ongoing work; like a blossoming garden, people and situations are constantly shifting and evolving. Your healing journey will be a continuous process as you move toward the future. In this final chapter, you will practice tending the garden of your relationship with your parent. You'll use new insights, strategies, and scripts to shift out of codependency and become more independent, practice firm and loving communication, and learn how not to get emotionally hooked while interacting with your parent. You will explore accountability and how you can practice being accountable, holding your parent accountable, setting consequences, and choosing reconciliation or less contact. No matter how you decide to progress your relationship with your parent, it will be based on what is best for your healing and happiness.

66 Supporting Each Other Without Rescuing

INDEPENDENCY VERSUS CODEPENDENCY

THERE IS A GOOD CHANCE that you learned from your emotionally imma-ture parent that codependency and enmeshment is what it means to love one another. Codependent and enmeshed relationships have two things in common: a lack of or weak boundaries and a lack of individual identity. Neither of these things nurtures a truly loving connection.

Codependent relationships feel one-sided. One person plays the res-cuer or caregiver (the enabler), believing that they must help or save the other person (the helpless) from their consequences and protect them from negative experiences. If you are in a codependent relationship with your parent, you might ignore your own problems and take on their problems while allowing them to over-rely on you for help. It's difficult for codepen-dents to separate their own needs, feelings, and the results of their actions from the other person. Addictions and poor behaviors can be excused, minimized, and ignored. Feelings of resentment, exhaustion, unfairness, and being taken advantage of tend to build.

Here's HOW If you want to be independent, you will need to shift your rela-tionship out of codependency. This will involve setting certain boundaries with your parent. If you're able to move through this process from a place of love, empathy, and calmness, it'll make it easier for your parent to recognize that people can be individuals while also being a family.

Put It Into PRACTICE

Here are examples of healthy boundaries you can set right now in order to shift out of a codependent relationship:

- Be clear with how you will *support* them instead of doing things *for* them.

- Don't tolerate poor behaviors. Address problems that you see.

- Take care of yourself and make sure that you're getting your needs met.

- Don't overextend yourself and try to rescue them from their problems—especially when they haven't even asked for help.

- Broaden your support system and don't only rely on one person to be your one and only everything.

- Be honest with how their codependent behaviors make you feel.

Remember:

- Codependent relationships feel one-sided.

- Codependent relationships involve a confusion of personal responsibilities, enabling poor behaviors, and fixing and rescuing other people from their problems.

- Take responsibility for taking care of your own needs and your well-being.

- Allow others to take responsibility for taking care of their needs and their well-being.

- Resolve codependency by setting boundaries, like supporting each other instead of doing things for each other and making sure your own needs are met.

67 | Being Together As Your Own Person
INDEPENDENCE VERSUS ENMESHMENT

IN ENMESHED RELATIONSHIPS, INDEPENDENCE AND differences are not allowed. Both people have to think the same, feel the same, and want the same. Physical and emotional space is limited. There is no "agree to disagree." If you try to have your own life outside of the relationship, set boundaries, think or feel differently, or try to make changes in the relationship, they may feel threatened and abandoned. And they might react to these feelings by rejecting you.

Here's HOW If you want to shift your relationship from one of enmeshment to one of individual freedom, it will take setting certain boundaries. And like with codependency, if you approach this issue with love, empathy, and calmness, your parent is more likely to realize that people can be unique and different while also being a family.

Put It Into PRACTICE Here are examples of healthy boundaries you can set right now to shift out of an enmeshed relationship:

- Focus on the quality of time together versus the quantity of time.

- Cultivate other relationships, have separate hobbies and interests, and be part of other groups.

- Be mindful of your urge for constant contact with them. Allow physical, mental, and emotional space in the relationship. It's okay to not *always* be thinking about them.

- Express your genuine thoughts and feelings.

- Be mindful of oversharing. Respect the other person's boundaries by checking if it's a good time and place for them before you share.

Write down your observations.

_____

_____

_____

_____

_____

_____

_____

_____

_____

_____

_____

_____

_____

Remember:

- Enmeshment is not real love.

- Enmeshed relationships involve blurred boundaries and expectations to think, feel, and want the same; individuality and a life outside of the relationship is not allowed.

- Setting clear boundaries, like expressing your genuine thoughts and feelings, standing up for your individuality, and cultivating other relationships is how you can resolve enmeshment.

68 Navigating Through the Growing Pains

FIRM AND LOVING COMMUNICATION

YOU WILL BE ROCKING THE boat as you're changing, healing, setting boundaries, and asking for what you want and need. Others may not see these changes as the positive changes they are. An emotionally immature parent will often struggle with handling change and the emotional discomforts of change. Also, they might perceive these changes where you're reclaiming your independence and calling for respect as disobedience, rejection, and/or abandonment. The secret to bringing the boat back to stability is this: firm and loving communication.

Here's HOW You want to speak from a place of love and have a firmness in your communication—finding the balance between soft and rigid. You don't want to be too soft, where it's easy to make you change your mind and take advantage of you. You also don't want to be too rigid, where it's either your way or the highway. You want to be firm and also flexible: clear and unwavering with your loving intentions and willing to compromise, negotiate, and make exceptions.

Put It Into PRACTICE Here's how to infuse your communication with firmness and love:

1. Be as clear and simple as possible with your words.

2. Repeat your words throughout their negative reactions.

3. Focus on maintaining calm and love for yourself and for them throughout every interaction.

4. Remind yourself that you won't be perfect at this and every interaction will give you more experience and build your emotional resilience.

5. Remember that their reaction is more about them and their emotional history and traumas than about you and the situation at hand.

6. Include words of empathy, understanding, and love in your communication. For example, "I love you mom and I'm not changing my mind" and "I still want to spend time with you, and I have other relationships that are also important to me."

Before following these steps, you can ask yourself these questions to prepare for loving and firm communication:

● What are some issues in the relationship that I need to address?

_____

_____

_____

_____

_____

● What are some of the things that are happening in the relationship that I need to give thanks for?

_____

_____

_____

_____

_____

- How can I communicate with more love?

_____

_____

_____

_____

_____

- How can I seek better understanding of their perspective (even if I might not get the same understanding back from them)?

_____

_____

_____

_____

_____

Remember:

- Even though a change may be positive, others might not perceive it this way.

- Emotionally immature parents can struggle with handling change and the uncomfortable emotions involved with it.

- You want to be firm, flexible, and loving when it comes to communication.

69 Handling a Conversation That Isn't Productive

WHEN IT COMES TO COMMUNICATING with your emotionally immature parent and other emotionally immature adults, there will be times when a productive conversation just isn't happening. Either you're emotionally triggered and reactive or they're emotionally triggered and reactive. If you and/or they have lost control of emotions and are in a reactive state, you may be able to bring the conversation back to a calm and effective place by detaching from these negative emotions.

Here's HOW There are two techniques that you can use to prevent you from getting hooked by your parent's reactivity as you enter a conversation with them or to "unhook" yourself if you've already been caught up in their emotions:

1. **The invisible glass window:** Imagine that there is a glass window that separates you from the other person. Their emotional reaction doesn't come through the glass. Note what you see and hear as you're observing them through this "window."

2. **The gray rock technique:** Imagine that you're a smooth, gray rock that's made it through the roughest challenges that nature has thrown at you. The other person's words are like gusts of wind that don't harm you.

Put It Into PRACTICE The next time you're having a conversation with your parent or other emotionally immature adult and you notice that one or both of you are getting reactive and have lost your cool, try these techniques and see which works best for you. (Maybe both together work best for you!)

Write down your observations.

_____

_____

_____

_____

_____

_____

_____

_____

_____

_____

_____

_____

Remember:

● Communication with emotionally immature parents and other emotionally immature adults can be difficult.

● The invisible glass window and gray rock technique are two ways you can maintain calm while not getting hooked on (or unhook from) their emotional reactions.

● Sometimes, one technique may resonate more than the other, or you may find that using both works best for you.

70 Handling a Conversation That Has Escalated

TAKING A TIME-OUT

THERE WILL BE CONVERSATIONS WHERE, even after trying these techniques, the situation escalates to unproductive yelling, pointless arguing, emotionally shutting down, etc. If a calm and productive conversation isn't possible, then you can pause the conversation and return to it at another time.

Here's HOW Pausing a conversation when it has become aggressive and unproductive is the mature and responsible thing to do. Becoming aware of when you and/or the other person are starting to lose control of your emotions is the first step. If you feel threatened, scared, or overwhelmed, it's time to pause the conversation. If you are emotionally shutting down or you notice the other person shutting down, it's time to pause the conversation. If you feel you are not in control of your anger, it's time to pause the conversation.

Put It Into PRACTICE Here are the steps that you can take if you need to pause a conversation:

1. Stop communicating and take a few deep breaths.

2. Express the need for a pause. Use "I" statements to share how you feel and suggest taking a break from the conversation. For example, "I'm feeling overwhelmed right now, and I think we both need a break."

3. Recommend a break of 10–15 minutes or however much time you feel you need. For example, "Let's take a 10-minute break to calm down."

4. Schedule a follow-up. Agree to continue the conversation when emotions have settled. For example, "Can we continue this conversation once we're both in a calmer place and have had the chance to reflect on things?"

5. Shift the focus temporarily. Redirect the conversation to a neutral topic to diffuse tension. For example, "While we take a break from this…what shall we eat for supper?"

6. Use your body language to communicate. Step back or sit down to signal the need for a pause.

7. Set communication boundaries. Remind the other person about the importance of respectful discussion when you are ready to talk about the issue. For example, "I understand we have strong opinions, but next time let's try to talk about this without yelling or arguing. Can we agree to communicate respectfully?"

8. Listen actively. When you return to the conversation, listen, then summarize the other person's viewpoint and ask for clarification to demonstrate your understanding. For example, "So what I hear you saying is [their point]. Is that correct?"

9. Seek external support. Involve a neutral third party, such as a therapist or mediator, if needed.

Remember:

- When a conversation is becoming aggressive, unproductive, or overwhelming, it's time for a pause.

- Calmly express your feelings and suggest taking a short break to cool down.

- Schedule a follow-up and agree to continue the conversation later when emotions have settled.

- Practice active listening and seek support by summarizing the other person's viewpoint, clarify misunderstandings, and consider involving a neutral third party if necessary.

71 Working Through Conflicts and Confrontations

A GUIDED MEDITATION IN RELATIONSHIP ISSUES

IT'S INEVITABLE TO EXPERIENCE MISUNDERSTANDINGS, differences in opinions and expectations, and wrong assumptions in your relationships. Especially in a relationship with an emotionally immature parent. Growing up, you might've observed that confrontations and conflicts often (or always) led to yelling, fighting, and maybe even violence. But it doesn't have to go this way. You can take a vulnerable approach when confronting your parent and increase your chances of moving through the conflict with both sides having a greater understanding of each other and working together to find a solution.

Here's HOW You learned about the vulnerable conversation framework in Activity 47: Building Communication. Now you're going to use this framework as a guide in confronting your parent about a present issue. You can use the first three parts of this framework to open up a conversation. If your parent is still incapable of productively and peacefully moving through the conflict with you, then in part four you can let them know exactly what you want and need instead.

Put It Into PRACTICE In this practice, you will move through the vulnerable conversation framework using a guided meditation provided at EmotionallyImmatureParents.com. If you don't want to practice the guided meditation or don't have access to the website, you can instead identify an issue that's happening in your relationship with your parent now and use the space provided to go through the four parts of the framework:

1. What is it that they're doing? What is it that they're saying? For example, maybe your mom is telling you to be sure the oven is turned off after you use it.

_____

_____

2. How do these words and actions make you feel? For example, your mom's reminders are making you feel like you aren't trustworthy with adult tasks like using the oven.

_____

_____

3. What is your interpretation of their words/actions? For example, that your mom thinks you are a helpless child rather than an adult.

4. What do you want? What do you need? For example, for them to stop reminding you of the things you already know.

5. Use your insights from the framework to guide you as you share your observations, feelings, wants, and needs with your parent.

Remember:

● Conflicts occur in all relationships, even healthy ones.

● Conflicts and confrontations don't necessarily lead to arguing, fighting, or violence.

● Confrontations mean that you respect and value yourself and your boundaries and that you also value honesty and the relationship, so you're willing to bring up an issue.

● Conflicts and confrontations can be done productively and even peacefully.

● Confrontations and moving through conflicts can bring both sides together with greater understanding by dealing with an issue together and moving toward a solution together.

72 Rebuilding Trust

THE VULNERABLE CONFRONTATION FRAMEWORK

In Activity 48: Building Trust from Within, you used the BRAVING method to build self-trust and determine whether another person may be trustworthy. Trust isn't something you can build and then forget about; strengthening and maintaining it takes consistency and dedication. As you go through life, you will likely experience different degrees of broken trust, which will require different degrees of effort in rebuilding. For example, your dad showing up 20 minutes late for lunch occasionally can impact the trust in the relationship to a small degree compared to your mom revealing a personal secret to another family member.

Here's HOW You can confront your parent about broken trust using the vulnerable conversation framework explored earlier in Part 3. Then, to start rebuilding that broken trust, you can practice forgiveness, letting go of the past, processing any negative emotions that came up regarding what happened, and reminding and holding each other accountable.

Put It Into PRACTICE

1. **Confront:** Initiate the conversation and share with them what you noticed, how it made you feel, and the storyline in your head. Ask them to talk to you about it.

2. **Forgive:** Affirmations that you can use in this step are: "I forgive them for what happened," "I let go of the past to be here today," "It will take some time to trust them again," and "We will work together and remind each other." Repeat the affirmation(s) that resonates with you frequently.

3. **Process negative emotions:** You'll likely encounter difficult emotions like abandonment, betrayal, hurt, disappointment, and jealousy following whatever happened. Going through the RAIN process introduced in Part 2 can help you process these feelings.

4. **Be patient:** Be patient with yourself and even ask for their patience as both of you are rebuilding the trust. Asking for their patience can sound like, "Please give me time and space to go through the difficult emotions that are coming up from what happened. I want to trust you again. This relationship matters to me. Please be patient with me."

Remember:

- Trust is not something you can build and then be done with.

- Your trust can be broken to different degrees depending on what happened.

- Trust takes time, effort, honesty, consistency, and dedication to rebuild.

- Rebuilding trust will require a vulnerable conversation, practicing forgiveness, processing negative emotions, and being patient with yourself and with them.

Moving Forward Together

RECONCILIATION

YOU'VE BEEN DISCOVERING WHO YOU really are, gaining independence, and healing yourself through the activities in this workbook. This is how you can help your parent heal: by helping yourself. You know you can't make your parent change or force them to recognize that they're hurting and they also need to heal. However, with your healing and changing, you can encourage and inspire them to heal and make changes too. If it's what you want to do, you can take steps toward reconciliation.

Here's HOW You'll have to lead the way by initiating a compassionate conversation with your parent. Because you've been healing and freeing yourself from the anger, fear, and mistrust that you've inherited from your parent, you are better able to see similar suffering inside of them. Can you see them as an imperfect human? Can you speak lovingly to the wounded inner child that lives inside of them and ask them to move forward with you in reconciliation? The conversation won't be perfect (nothing is). Just try your best; it will be good enough.

Put It Into PRACTICE Write out what you want to say in this conversation, then practice saying it to yourself or a trusted friend before talking to your parent. Here's an example of initiating reconciliation to help get you started: "Mom, I know you've been hurting for so long now. I'm sorry that I haven't been able to help you hurt any less and I might've even added to your hurting. I've been reacting out of my feelings of anger, hurt, fear, stubbornness, and loneliness. I didn't mean to hurt you. I didn't understand the pain inside of me, and I couldn't see the pain that lives inside of you. Mom, can you please tell me what's going on inside of you? Can you help me understand your anger, your fear, and your pain? So that I can better understand you and try my best to not say or do anything that will make you hurt more? I want to help heal and grow our relationship. But I need you to talk to me. I can't do this without you."

Remember:

- The best way that you can help your parent is by helping yourself first.

- Throughout this workbook, you've been healing and releasing the anger, fear, and mistrust that you might've inherited from your family.

- You can inspire your parent to release the same anger, fear, and mistrust.

- If it fits your goals, you can initiate a compassionate conversation with your parent in order to work toward reconciliation.

74 Moving Forward Separately

ULTIMATUMS AND LIMITED CONTACT

YOU LEARNED THAT RESPECT MEANS knowing, seeing, and accepting someone just as they are, not as you want them to be. When it comes to your
relationship with your parent, mutual respect might be missing as they're
seeing you from the lens of their expectations of you. They might even
believe they know what's best for you without considering your perspective.
If you've tried setting boundaries, consistently letting them know when
you're feeling disrespected by their words and actions, and you've asked for
change, letting them know that you need them to respect your decisions
and opinions, then it's time to respect yourself.

Here's HOW Respect yourself by choosing to spend less time with them. Issue
an ultimatum to go limited contact or even no contact. This
doesn't have to be permanent, as people and situations can change, but it
may be what is best for your healing for the time being. While no contact
means just that, limited contact could mean anything from no talking
about topics where you can't agree to disagree on. Or not answering certain questions. It can be you choosing to initiate less. Or saying no sometimes to spending time together. How you limit contact or whether you
choose no contact is up to you and what will help you heal.

Put It Into PRACTICE

1. How much time do you want to spend with your parent?

_____

_____

2. What topics are you willing to talk about? What topics and questions are you not willing to talk about?

3. When will you revisit your level of contact with your parent? When they are willing to show you more respect? After you have had some time to focus on self-care?

4. What will you say to communicate this ultimatum? For example, "Hey Mom and Dad, I'm exhausted. I've tried many times to let you know I don't like it when you _____ and it makes me feel disrespected. I'm going to be spending [less time/no time] with you, at least for a while, because I don't want to feel this way anymore.

Remember:

- Mutual respect is a key ingredient in a healthy relationship.

- You can't make people respect you, but you can choose to respect yourself.

- If you've tried setting boundaries, consistently addressing the issue, and setting consequences and your parent still chooses to mistreat you, then issuing an ultimatum can be the next step.

- Going no contact or limited contact is how you can choose to respect yourself when you are not being respected by your parent.

Additional Book Resources

The following are books that have helped me immensely in my own journey of self-discovery and healing. I recommend them to help you continue the path to recovery and dig even deeper into the aspects of healing that resonate with you most, including childhood wounds; emotional maturity; healthy and firm boundaries; respectful, loving, and supportive relationships; and living a life that's true to you.

Adult Children of Emotionally Immaturate Parents: How to Heal from Distant, Rejecting, or Self-Involved Parents by Lindsay C. Gibson, PsyD

I highly encourage you to pick up a copy of this book as soon as possible and read it several times. Lindsay C. Gibson is a clinical psychologist who reveals how emotionally immature parents negatively impact their children. She identifies the long-term negative effects and adult issues caused by such a childhood and also how to heal and move through the pain, confusion, and loneliness. You'll learn how to free yourself from your parent's emotional immaturity, discover who you really are, and interact with your parent with less reactivity.

Boundaries: When to Say Yes, How to Say No to Take Control of Your Life by Dr. Henry Cloud and Dr. John Townsend

This is a classic book on boundaries written by two therapists who've been helping clients set boundaries for decades. Learn powerful frameworks and scripts to begin setting healthy boundaries in all areas of your life and across different relationships, like those with family, friends, your career, and social media/technology.

Healing the Shame That Binds You by John Bradshaw

In this powerful, healing book by John Bradshaw, learn more about how toxic shame gets passed down from generation to generation and how it influences unhealthy behaviors, like addictions, compulsions, codependency, and perfectionism. This book offers you healing and shame-releasing techniques so you can let go of any toxic shame at the root of your personal and relationship issues.

Homecoming: Reclaiming and Healing Your Inner Child by John Bradshaw

Learn about inner child healing and how to connect, champion, and reparent the wounded inner child that's living inside of you. In this important book, John Bradshaw offers you a step-by-step process to become the loving and protective parent that you always needed and longed for.

Set Boundaries, Find Peace: A Guide to Reclaiming Yourself by Nedra Glover Tawwab

Nedra Glover Tawwab offers a guide on setting boundaries for better work-life balance, dealing with toxic behaviors, and cultivating more respect in all your relationships so that you can enjoy them more. Also, make sure to follow her *Instagram* account for daily doses of practical wisdom on boundaries and healthy relationships.

"The Guest House," *The Rumi Collection* by Jalaluddin Rumi

This poem is the inspiration for Activity 11: Understanding the Full Spectrum of Emotions.

Unf*ck Your Boundaries: Build Better Relationships Through Consent, Communication, and Expressing Your Needs by Faith G. Harper, PhD, LPC-S, ACS, ACN

A short, succinct, and practical read, this book by Dr. Faith G. Harper teaches you the importance of boundaries, the common issues around boundaries and consent, and how to effectively communicate your boundaries, ask for help, and express your needs. She offers simple strategies, powerful frameworks, and scripts for you to navigate through conflicts, respect your own and other people's boundaries, and get better results in your relationships.

Online Resources for Mental Health Support

The following are resources that I've found helpful along the path to recovery from emotionally immature parents. You may wish to use them as additional support as you work through this book or to continue your journey beyond these pages.

BetterHelp

www.betterhelp.com
An affordable and accessible way to work with licensed therapists online, this is the world's largest therapy service. There's a short form that you fill out initially to help match you with a therapist who fits your needs and preferences.

Co-Dependents Anonymous

www.coda.org
This resource offers online and in-person support groups for recovering from codependency. They provide a structured, step-by-step approach to guide you out of codependent relationships into healthy and loving relationships. They also have a free newsletter that you can sign up for on their website.

Headspace

Headspace is an app that helps meditation practitioners of all levels and lifestyles develop a regular practice. It offers various types and lengths of meditations to fit your needs. There are fun, educational animated videos that teach you how to meditate if you are on a more beginner level.

My *Instagram* and *TikTok* Accounts

www.instagram.com/hicoachkai/
www.tiktok.com/@hicoachkai
I post daily educational videos on the topics covered in this workbook. I often host *Instagram* and *TikTok* Lives that are educational, interactive, and engaging. You can also join my free newsletter through either of these accounts and be the first to find out about upcoming virtual events and master classes.

Psychology Today

www.psychologytoday.com
Psychology Today offers hundreds of useful articles focused on psychology and human behavior. These articles are written by psychologists, doctors, social workers, and science journalists. The website also features a directory for finding therapists and healthcare professionals in your area if you live in the US.

Tara Brach's Podcast

Tara Brach, PhD, is a world-renowned meditation teacher and author of bestselling books, *Radical Acceptance* and *True Refuge*. Her teachings on mindfulness, compassion, and acceptance and her guided meditations are practical resources you can supplement as you complete this workbook. She offers a holistic approach, mixing Western psychology with Eastern spiritual wisdom and practices.

Index